Copyright © 1997 Susan Scheewe Publications Inc.
13435 N.E. Whitaker Way - Portland, Or. 97230
PH(503)254-9100 Fax (503)252-9508

Dear Paintin' Pals,

These projects were fun to do and they look sooo cute on my porch. I know they will on your's too! Painting has been a fun hobby for me. The best part is the new friends I make at conventions. I look forward to seeing you each year. Thanks for your support.

I am grateful for my family. They teach me so much about life and living. Thank you family, for your support, love and strength. A big thanks to Curtis and Carrie Rasmussen, my woodcutters! Especially, thanks to everyone at Susan Scheewe Publications! You have all been patient and great.

Happy Paintin'!

Love, Vickie

The wood projects in this book were cut and provided by:

C&R WOODS
PO Box 694
Kaysville, UT 84037
1-801-451-7916

Plum Fun Wood Products
5427 S.E. 72nd Avenue
Portland, OR 97206
1-503-777-3351

Brushes provided by:

Loew-Cornell
563 Chestnut Avenue
Teaneck, NJ 07666-2490
1-201-836-7070

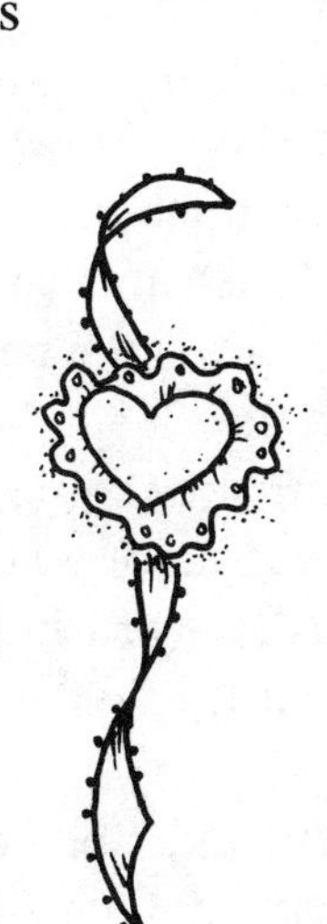

Pens Provided By:

Pigma Micron
30780 San Clemente St.
Hayward, CA 94544
(510) 475-8880

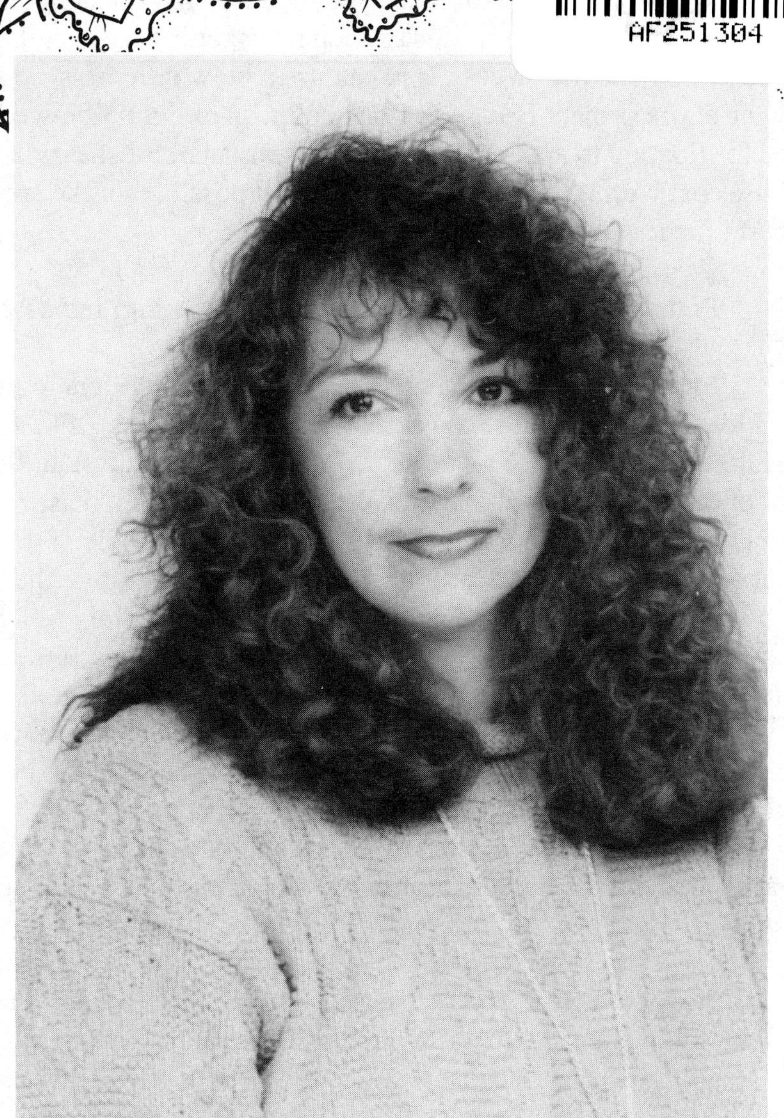

GENERAL DIRECTIONS

Wood Preparation: Sand the wood well. Use a tack cloth to remove all traces of sawdust. Seal the wood. When dry, lightly sand and tack again.

Paint: When the directions ask to mix two colors together use equal amounts of paint unless a ratio is given. For example, White + Black (3:1). This means mix 3 drops of the first color + 1 drop of the second color.

Wash: To base wood using a wash, keep the paint very sheer (one part paint to six parts water). You should be able to see the wood grain beneath the wash.

Base Coating: Try to keep your strokes smooth and going with the wood grain. Base in just a hair away from the pattern edge to keep from getting a ridge of paint. Several light layers of base coat is better than one heavy coat. You can use a blow dryer to speed up the drying process between coats. If your entire project is based in one color, sand lightly between base coats. Don't use your brushes used for floating to apply the base coat. Your detail brushes will last much longer if you don't use them to base coat with. Always use the largest flat possible for the area to base with. I base round areas with filbert brushes.

Peppering: The dots on the pattern (peppering) indicate shadow placement.

Float Shade and **Float Highlight**: This term refers to the shading and highlighting of a color. To "Float Shade" is a side load float of the shadow color. "Float Highlight" refers to a side load float of the highlight color. I use a #12 or 1/2" flat brush for almost all floating. Always use the largest flat you can for the area you are working. Wet the brush and blot on several thicknesses of a good quality paper towel until the brush looses its "wet gloss." Load one side of the brush about 1/3 of the way over in the paint and blend back and forth on your palette to distribute the paint to the center of the brush. Blend both sides of your brush, keeping one side clean. Lightly touch the "loaded" brush on a wet spot on your paper towel to avoid a beginning harsh line of color. If the brush becomes dry as you are floating, touch the corner of the brush containing the water into a small puddle of water that you've placed on your palette, lightly blend and float again. It isn't necessary to wash the brush each time you reload into the same color. Good blending on the palette is the secret to beautiful floats.

Layering Float Colors: When the directions say to float shade then deepen in another color, float shade with the darker color only in the areas that would be the darkest. Do not refloat the entire area.

Reverse Float: This is used to highlight the center of an object. Load the brush the same as for a float. Float one side then flip the brush over and float next to the first float.

Stipple Highlight: Loew Cornell Fabric Dye brushes are the best brushes for this technique. Keep the brush as dry as possible. Load the brush and then pounce it up and down on the palette to blend. Pounce on the paper towel to remove almost all of the paint from the brush. When you think that most of the paint is on the paper towel you are ready to stipple your wood. Keep turning the brush to avoid getting splotches. Don't overwork the area. Keep it light, letting the base color show through.

Palette Blend Two Colors: Use this method to mix the colors together instead of mixing puddles of paint together on your palette. Dip the same corner of the brush into both colors of paint and then blend them together on the palette. Palette Blending saves time and paint if you only need a tiny amount of color.

Dolly Parton Hearts (or dip dot hearts): Dip the end of your brush into a fresh puddle of paint and place two dots side by side on your wood. Use a liner or the end of a stylus to pull the center of the heart down.

Line work: When using paint to do the line work, thin the paint with water so the paint will flow freely from the liner. For most of my line work I prefer to use a pen.

Sponge Technique: Natural Sea Sponges can be purchased at craft or art stores. Because no two sponges are alike, everyone's project will look different. Sponging is fast and a lot of fun to do. A small sponge, 2" or 3" in diameter works best for most projects. Wet the sponge in clean water then wring it out. Dip part of the sponge into the paint then blot out most of the paint onto a paper towel. Apply the sponge to the project making sure not to overwork a wet area. In other words, apply light layers of sponging, letting each layer dry between coats. Turn the sponge as you are working to avoid getting a pattern. Let the background color of each previous color show through on each layer to build definition and to emphasize shading and highlighting.

BRUSHES

It is very important to use good quality brushes for each step of your project. Save those "old" ones, they are great for basing! I love to use filberts for basing small rounded objects such as eyes.

LOEW-CORNELL
563 Chestnut Avenue
Teaneck, NJ 07666-2490
(201) 836-7070

For **Stippling**:
Fabric Dye #10, #4, #2

For **Line work**:
Jackie's 10/0 liner, #1
Rounds 7350 Series #0, #2

For **Floating**:
7350 Series #2
7300 Series #4, #6, #8, #12
7500 Filbert #4, #8
7550 Series 1/2

Pipe Cutting Directions for Bird Chimes and MistleToad Chimes

You need 35" of 1/2" copper pipe. Cut the pipe in the following lengths: 6", 6 1/2", 7", 7 1/2", and 8". Drill a small hole through each pipe about 1/2" down from the top. Spray as indicated. Attach the pipes with a double thickness of fishing line. I tied them on with square knots and tucked the tails into the pipe. Make sure the pipes are hanging level across the top.

Pipe Cutting Directions for 4th of July and Halloween Chimes

You will need 65" of 3/4" copper pipe. Cut the pipe into the following lengths: 11", 12", 13", 14" and 15". Drill a small hole through the top of each pipe about 3/4" down from the top. Spray as indicated and attach to the wood with a double thickness of fishing line. Tie them on with square knots and tuck the ends into the pipe. Make sure the pipes hang level across the top.

Wood Specifications

I used Home Decor Gel Wood Stain Maple by Delta to stain the wood pieces. I varnished with 3 coats of Exterior Varnish by Delta.

Weather Vane

1. Cut out of 3/4" wood a 10" diameter circle and router for base.
2. Cut 2 triangle base supports out of 1 1/2" wood. See pattern.
3. Cut the pole 19 3/4" long out of 1 1/2" x 1 1/2" wood.
4. Attach the base supports to the pole with wood screws then attach to the 10" diameter circle.
5. Cut 2 6" circles out of 3/4" wood and router the top piece. Attach the bottom circle to the pole. Drill a 1/2" hole half way through the top round piece
6. Cut a 3 1/4" circle out of 1 1/2" wood and router both the top and bottom. Drill a 1/2" hole half way through on the bottom and drill a 3/8" hole in the top. Drill 4, 3/8" holes on the sides.
7. Cut a 1/2" dowel 3 3/4" long.
8. Assemble the 6" circles with the Lazy Susan mechanism sandwiched in between. Lazy Susan mechanisms can be purchased at most hardware stores. Follow the manufactures assembly directions.
9. Insert the 1/2" dowel onto the top of the 6" circle and the bottom of the 3 3/4" circle.
10. Cut 3/8" doweling 1 1/2" long and wood glue into the top circle. The bottom center of all the base pieces have a 3/8" hole drilled in the center.
11. Cut 1/2" doweling into the following lengths:

Halloween Weather Vane	4 @ 5 5/8" long
Christmas Weather Vane	4 @ 2 1/4" long
Fourth of July Weather Vane	4 @ 5 3/8" long
Bird House Weather Vane	3 @ 6 1/8" long, 1 @ 4 1/8" long

Welcome Wood Specifications

1. Cut a 10" circle and router the top for a base.
2. Cut a pole 27 1/2" long out of 1 1/2" x 1 1/2" wood.
3. Cut four triangle supports and attach to the top and bottom of the pool with wood screws. See Pattern.
4. Drill a 1/2" hole in 3/4" from the sides of both top supports. See Pattern.
5. Cut two pieces of 1/2" dowel, 1 1/4" long and wood glue into top support holes.
6. Cut the bases for the Halloween Welcome, Christmas Welcome and Fourth of July Welcome 8" x 5" out of 3/4" wood and router. Measure in 1 3/4" from each side and drill two 1/2" holes half way through to the top. Drill a 3/8" hole in the top of each base. Cut 3/8" doweling 1 3/4" long and wood glue into the top of each base.
7. The Bird House base is 6" x 7". Measure in 1 3/8" from each side and drill two 1/2" holes half way through to the top. The side pieces of the bird house are 2 1/2" x 4 3/4". The top roof pieces are 3 7/8" x 5 1/2".

Painting directions for:

Bird House Welcome
Bird House Weather Vane
Bird Chimes

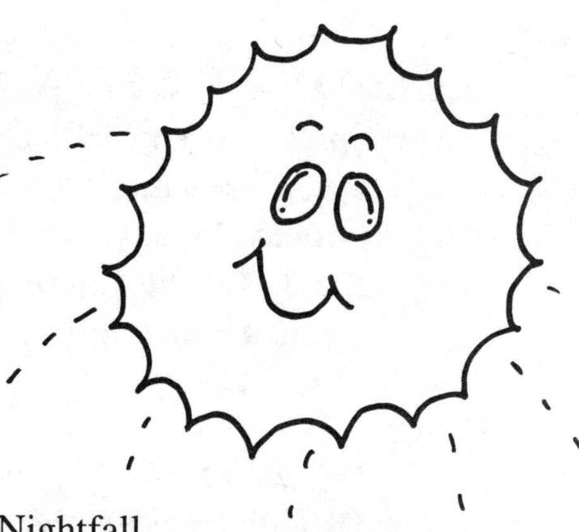

PALETTE (by Delta)

Spice Brown	Crocus	Drizzle Grey	Nightfall
Hunter Green	Lime Green	Cactus	Black Green
Blue Danube	Denim Blue	Midnight	Black
White	Bittersweet	Georgia Clay	Rose Mist
Barn Red	Sachet	Wild Rose	Putty
Burnt Umber	Hippo Grey		

Additional supplies needed for WELCOME:

Wood glue
10" of 19 gauge wire

Additional supplies needed for CHIMES:

Pipes
2' of 19 gauge wire
small amount of raffia
hot glue
fishing line
2 screw eyes
Krylon Brown Spray Paint

Additional supplies needed for WEATHER VANE:
Wood glue
10" of 19 gauge wire
1/4" picot ribbon
4 yds of pink and blue

Welcome Wedges Top & Bottom
(See Wood Preparations In General Directions)

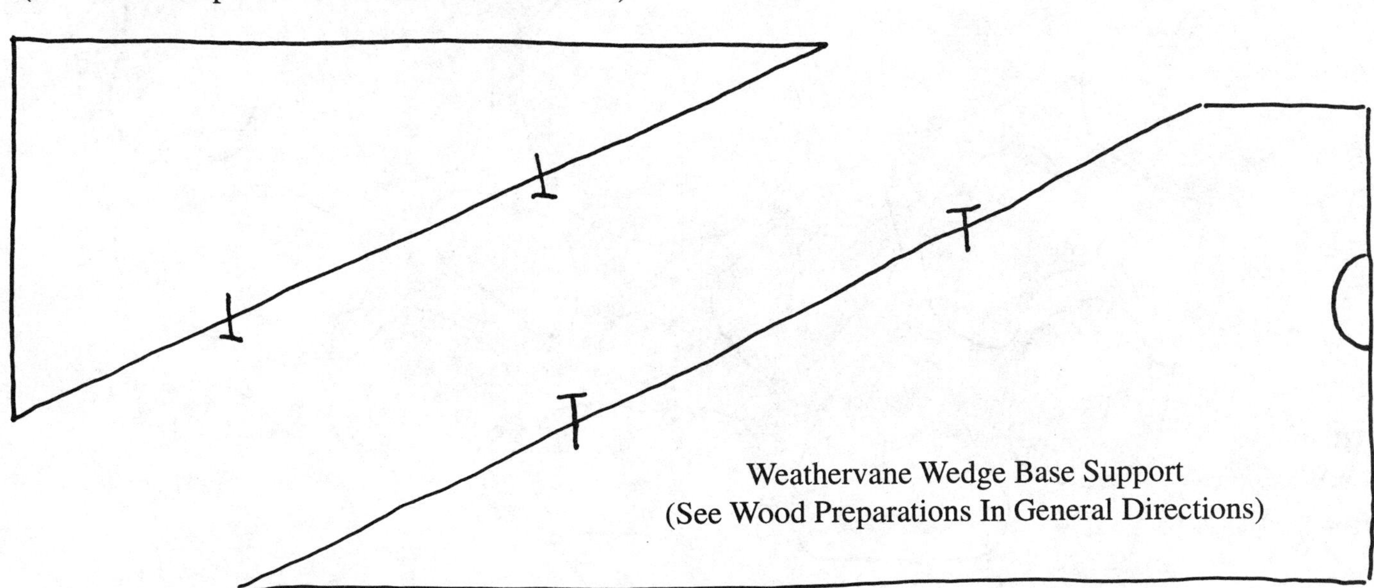

Weathervane Wedge Base Support
(See Wood Preparations In General Directions)

WELCOME and WEATHER VANE BIRDHOUSE ROOF

Spice Brown: Wash the roof, perch, and the base.
Spice Brown: Float shade.
Crocus: Float highlight.
Black: Do the lettering.
Burnt Umber: Fly speck the roof.

HOUSE

Drizzle Grey: Base the house.
Hippo Grey: Float Shade.

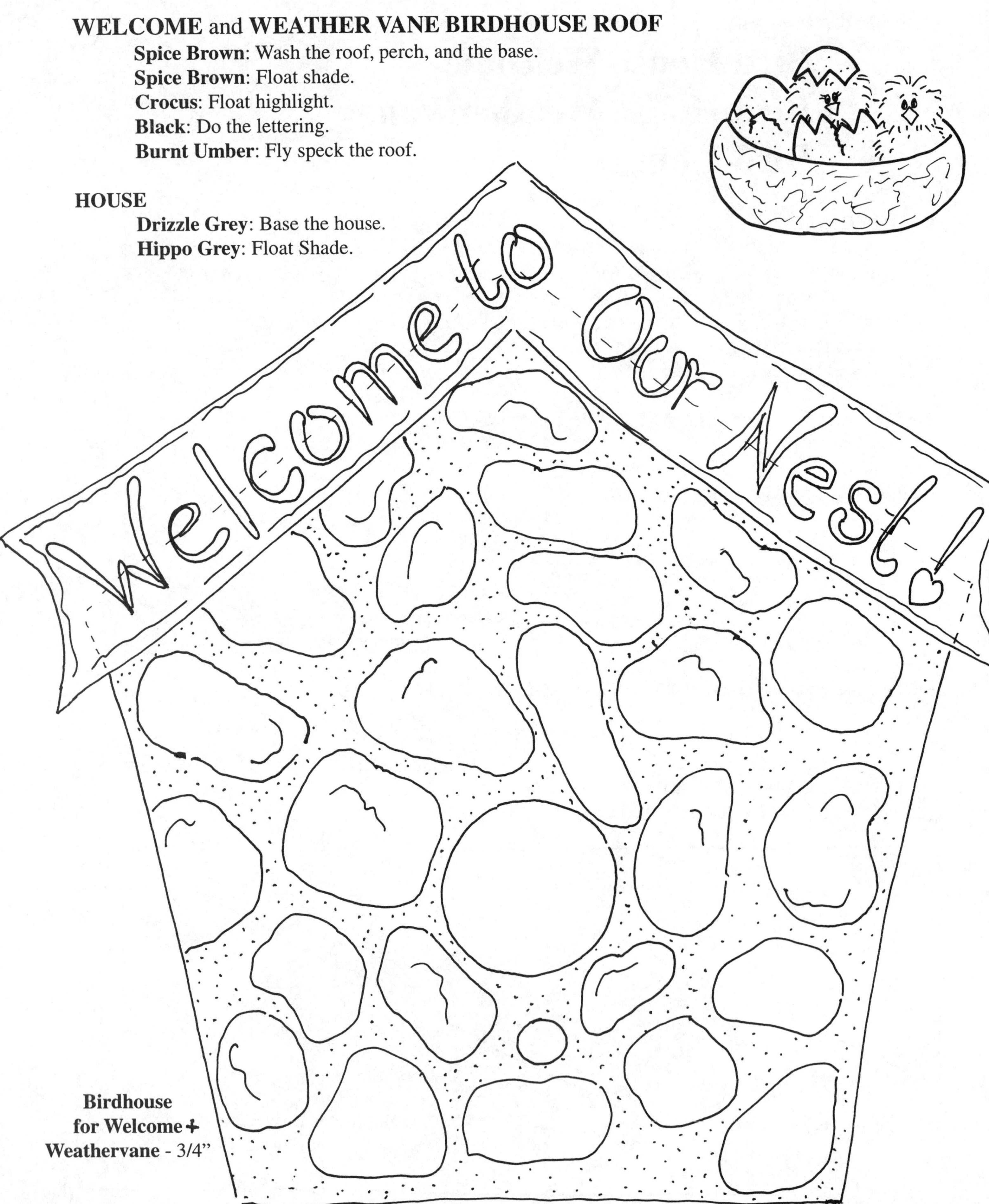

**Birdhouse
for Welcome ✛
Weathervane - 3/4"**

BUSHES

Hunter Green + Lime Green: Base the bushes.
Black Green: Float shade the bushes. Do **Black Green** and **Lime Green** crescent strokes.
Lime Green: Float highlight the tops of the bushes.
White: Use your stylus to do the little flowers.

BOW

Sachet + White: Base the bow.
Wild Rose: Float shade.
White: Float highlight.
Wild Rose: Do the pattern on the bow.

OPENING

Hippo Grey: Base the opening.
Black: Float Shade the opening.

ROCKS

Base some **Denim Blue**. Float shade **Midnight**. Float highlight **Blue Danube**.
Base some **Bittersweet**. Float shade **Georgia Clay**. Float highlight **White**.
Base some **Rose Mist**. Float shade **Barn Red**. Float highlight **White**.
Hippo Grey & **Black**: Float shade under the rocks.

FLY SPECK THE HOUSE

First with **Hippo Grey**, then with **White**.

WEATHER VANE BIRDS

Blue Danube: Base the birds.
White: Stipple the wings and body.
Denim Blue: Float shade and then deepen with **Midnight**.
Crocus + White: Base the beaks and feet.
Crocus + Bittersweet: Float shade the beaks and feet.
White: Stipple the center of the beak.
Barn Red: Stipple the cheeks.
Black: Base the eyes.

FLOWER

Sachet + White: Base the flower.
Wild Rose: Float shade.
White: Float highlight and stipple the center of the petals.
Crocus: Base the centers.
White: Stipple the center.
Crocus + Bittersweet: Float shade around the edge of the flower center.
Cactus: Base the leaf.
Hunter Green: Float shade the leaf.
Black Green: Deepen the **Hunter Green** float shade.
White: Float highlight the leaf.

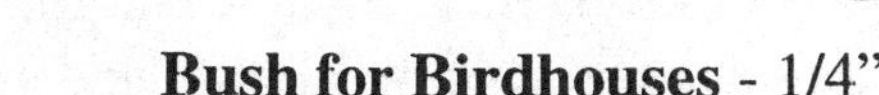

Bush for Birdhouses - 1/4"

Bird for Weathervane - 3/4"

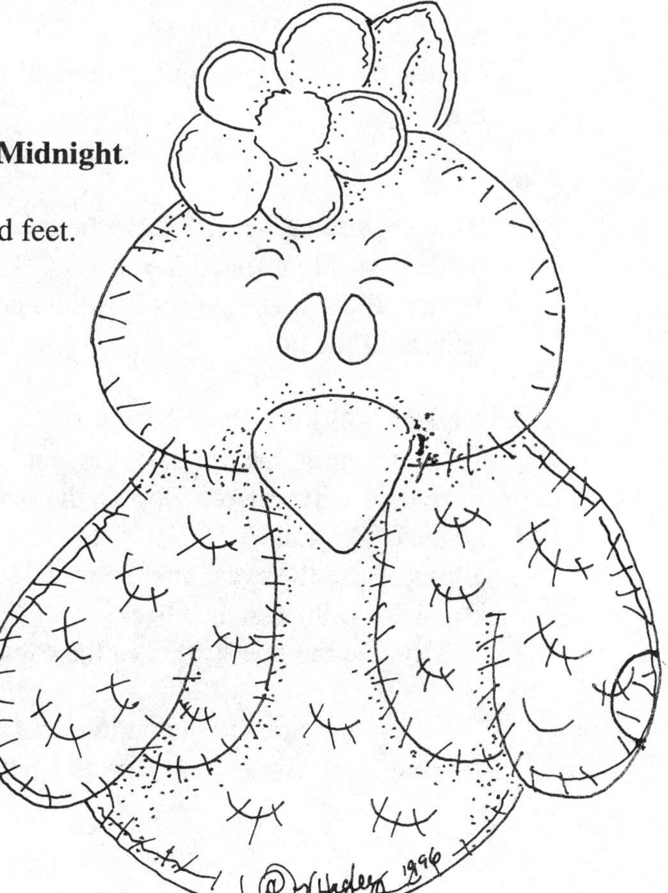

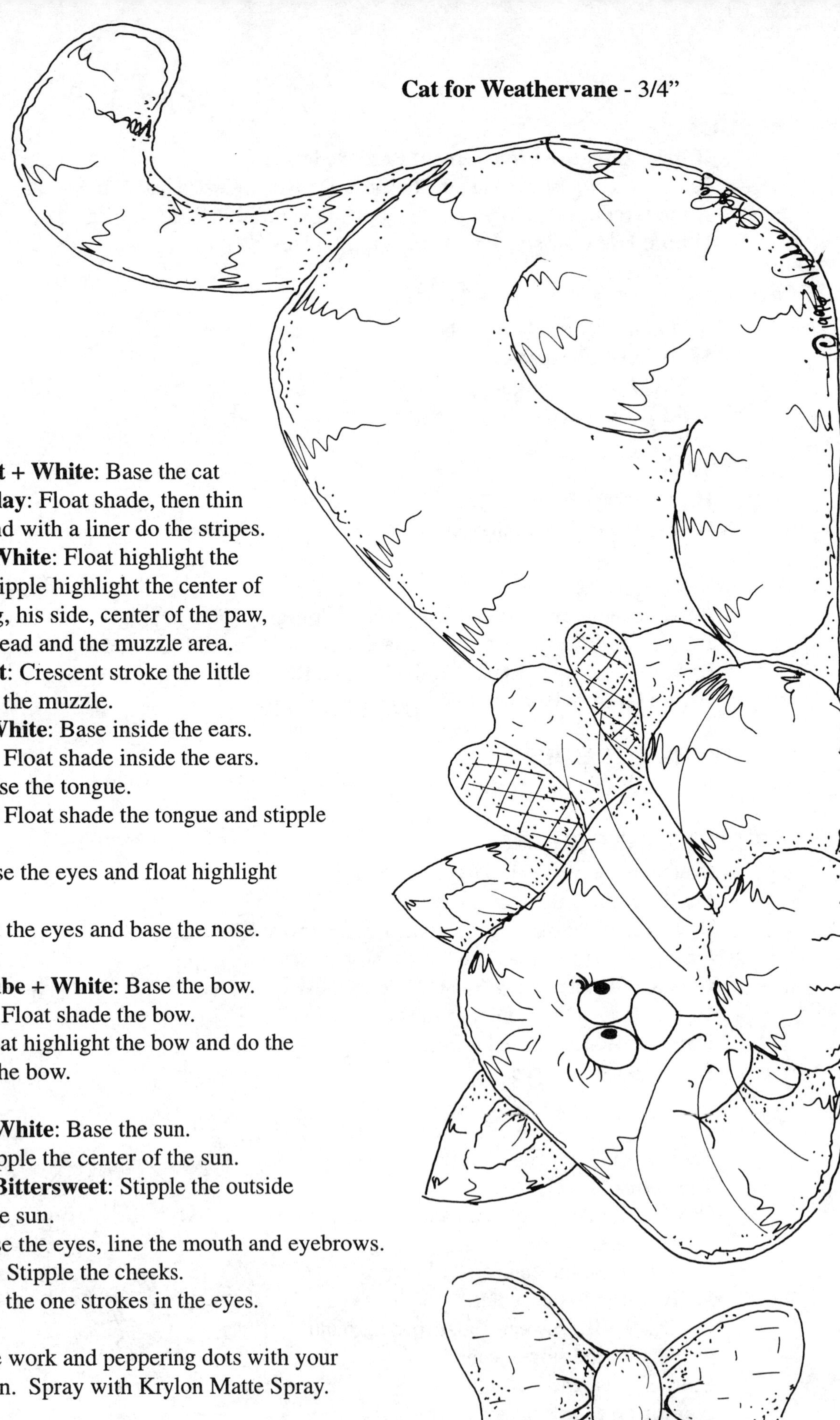

CAT

Bittersweet + White: Base the cat
Georgia Clay: Float shade, then thin the paint and with a liner do the stripes.
Crocus + White: Float highlight the ears then stipple highlight the center of the hind leg, his side, center of the paw, top of his head and the muzzle area.
Bittersweet: Crescent stroke the little dimples on the muzzle.
Sachet + White: Base inside the ears.
Barn Red: Float shade inside the ears.
Sachet: Base the tongue.
Barn Red: Float shade the tongue and stipple the cheeks.
White: Base the eyes and float highlight the tongue.
Black: Dot the eyes and base the nose.

BOW

Blue Danube + White: Base the bow.
Midnight: Float shade the bow.
White: Float highlight the bow and do the pattern in the bow.

SUN

Crocus + White: Base the sun.
White: Stipple the center of the sun.
Crocus + Bittersweet: Stipple the outside edges of the sun.
Black: Base the eyes, line the mouth and eyebrows.
Barn Red: Stipple the cheeks.
White: Do the one strokes in the eyes.

Do the line work and peppering dots with your favorite pen. Spray with Krylon Matte Spray.

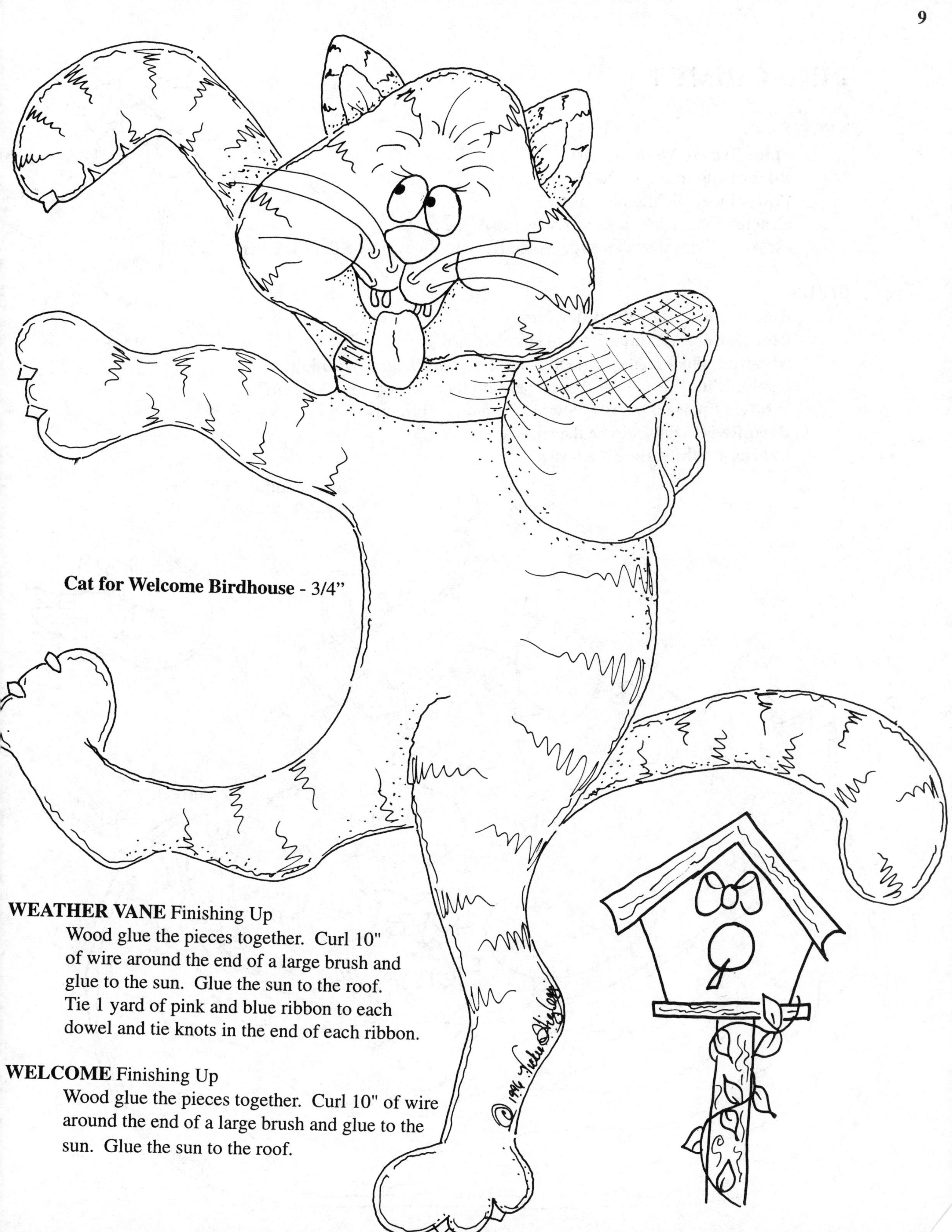

Cat for Welcome Birdhouse - 3/4"

WEATHER VANE Finishing Up
Wood glue the pieces together. Curl 10"
of wire around the end of a large brush and
glue to the sun. Glue the sun to the roof.
Tie 1 yard of pink and blue ribbon to each
dowel and tie knots in the end of each ribbon.

WELCOME Finishing Up
Wood glue the pieces together. Curl 10" of wire
around the end of a large brush and glue to the
sun. Glue the sun to the roof.

BIRD CHIMES

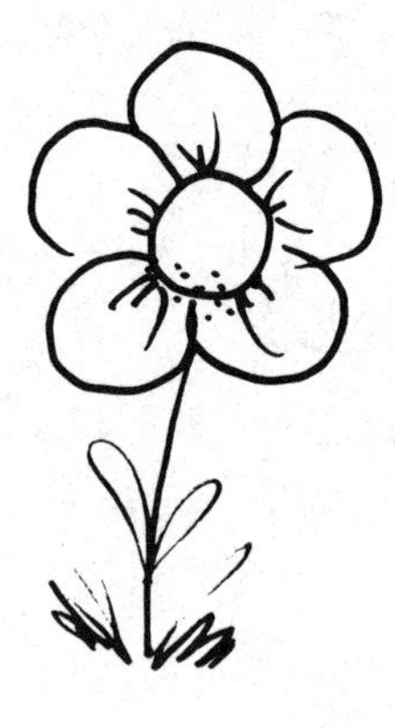

NEST

Spice Brown: Wash the nest.
Burnt Umber: Float Shade.
Putty: Float Highlight the nest.
Crocus: Float Highlight across the top of the nest.
Stroke individual straws with: **Spice Brown**, **Straw** and **Burnt Umber.**

BIRDS

Blue Danube: Base the daddy bird.
Blue Danube + White: Base the mother bird.
Nightfall: Float shade the daddy bird then deepen with **Midnight**.
Denim Blue: Float shade the mother bird then deepen with **Nightfall**.
White: Stipple both birds. Stipple the mother brightly.
Barn Red: Lightly stipple the cheeks.
Crocus + White: Base the beaks.

Bird Chime - 3/4"
Egg - 1/4"

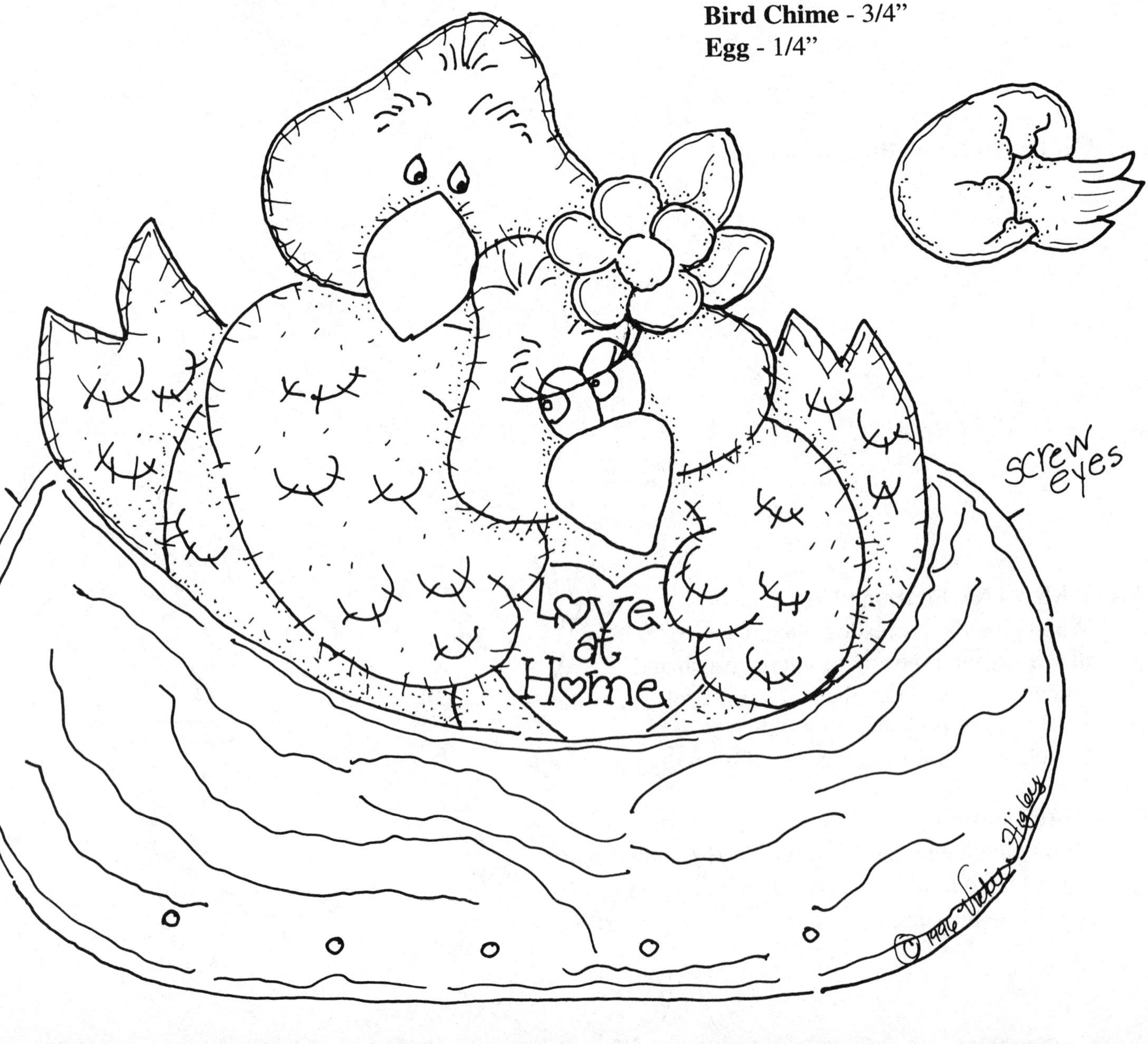

BIRD CHIMES Continued

Crocus + Bittersweet: Float shade the beaks.
White: Stipple the center of the beaks, base the mother bird's eyes and reverse float her eyelid.
Black: Base father's eyes, dot mother's pupil.
White: Dot the eyes.
Midnight: Float Shade mother's eyelash line.

HEART

Sachet + White: Base the heart.
White: Stipple the center of the heart.
Wild Rose: Float shade.
Barn Red: Deepen the float shade.

FLOWER

Wild Rose + White: Base the flower.
Wild Rose: Float shade.
White: Float highlight and stipple the center of each petal.
Barn Red: Deepen the float shade.
Crocus + White: Base the center.
White: Stipple the center.
Bittersweet: Float shade the center.
Cactus: Base leaves.
Hunter Green: Float shade the leaves.
Black Green: Deepen the float shade.
White: Float highlight the leaves.

Sun for birdhouses - 1/4"

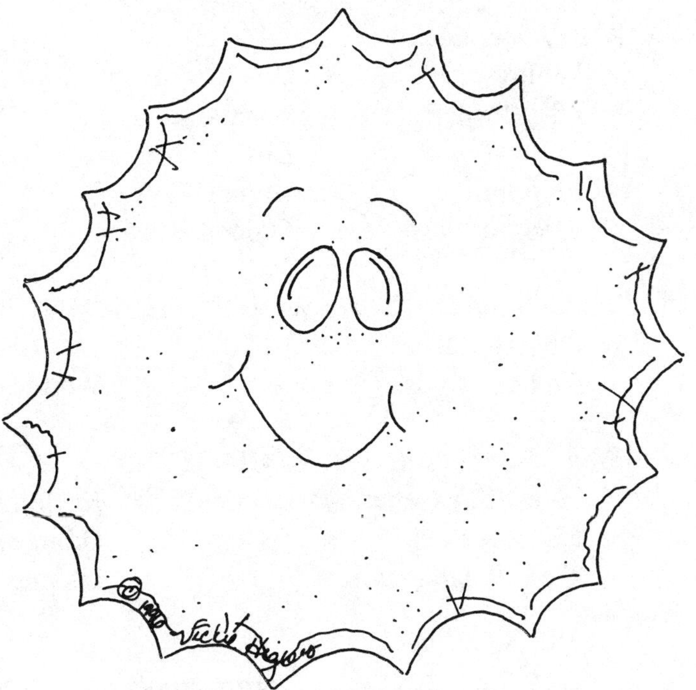

EGG

Putty: Base the egg.
Spice Brown: Float Shade the egg.
White: Float Highlight the egg. Fly Speck the egg **Denim Blue** then **Midnight**.

WING

Blue Danube: Base.
White: Stipple Highlight.
Denim Blue: Float Shade the wing.
Use your favorite pen for the line work.
Varnish with Krylon Matte Spray Finish

PIPES

Cut and assemble according to the General Directions. I sprayed the pipes with Krylon Brown Spray Paint. Attach the screw eyes to the wood where indicated. Curl the wire around the end of a large brush and thread through the screw eyes. Bend the ends around and cut off any extra wire. Tie a raffia bow and attach it to the wire. Hot glue the egg in place.

Painting Directions for:

Halloween Welcome
Halloween Weather Vane
Halloween Wind Chime

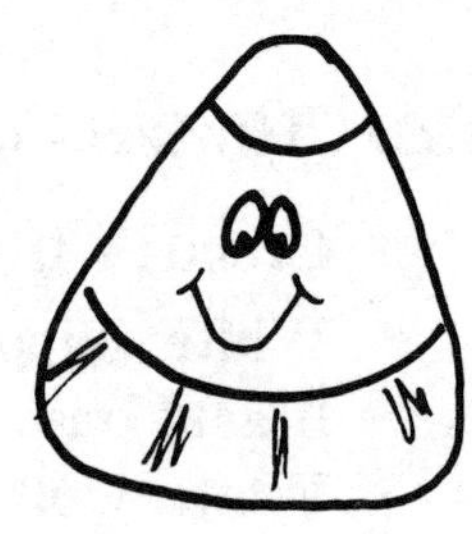

Does the witch remind you of a television detective? Clue - it rhymes with Dumbo.

PALETTE (by Delta)

White	Black	Blue Danube	Naphthol Crimson
Egg Plant	Fushia	Spice Brown	Burnt Umber
Yellow	Lime Green	Hunter Green	Tangerine
Pumpkin	Light Ivory	Crocus	Santa's Flesh
Medium Flesh	Golden Brown		

Additional Supplies Needed for **WEATHER VANE**:

Orange Raffia	1/4" Black Picot
Ribbon 4 yds	Wood Glue

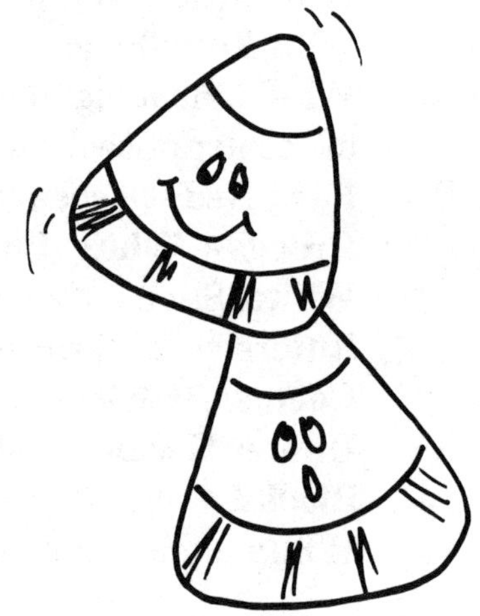

Additional Supplies needed for **CHIMES**:

Pipes (See General Directions)	Krylon Black Spray Paint
6 Screw eyes	Orange Raffia
2' of 19 gauge wire	Fishing line

Additional supplies needed for **WELCOME**:

3' of 19 gauge wire	
2 Black chenille stems cut into 3" lengths	Orange Raffia
1/8" dowel, 4" long	1/4" dowel, 7" long

GHOSTS

Blue Danube + White (1:5): Base the ghosts.

Blue Danube: Float shade the ghosts.

White: Stipple the bodies and float highlight the hair curls, fingers, tops of mouths, arms and reverse float the weathervane ghosts eyelids.

Naphthol Crimson: Base the nose of the weathervane ghost. Stipple all the cheeks.

White: Float highlight the top of the nose on the weathervane ghost. Base the weathervane ghost's eyes.

Black: Base the mouth and negative areas on the weathervane ghost. Dot the pupils or base the eyes. Outline the eyes and do eyelashes.

Egg Plant + White (1:4): Use a liner to do the bows. Base the large hair bow on the weathervane ghost.

Egg Plant: Float shade the large bow.

Midnight: Deepen the float shade on the bow.

Fushia + White (1:1): Stipple the highlights on the bow then float highlight.

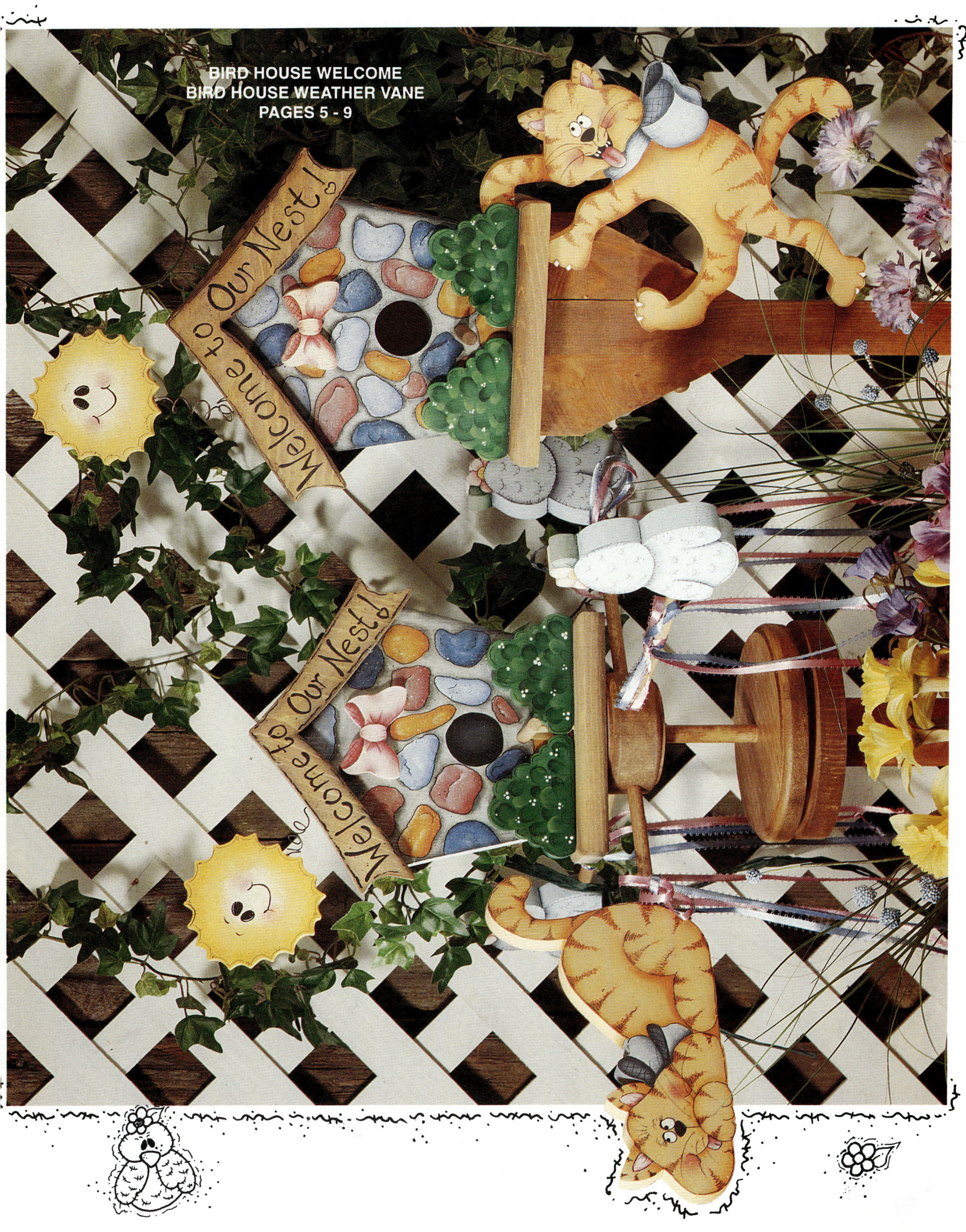

BIRD HOUSE WELCOME
BIRD HOUSE WEATHER VANE
PAGES 5 - 9

Welcome to Our Nest!
Welcome to Our Nest!

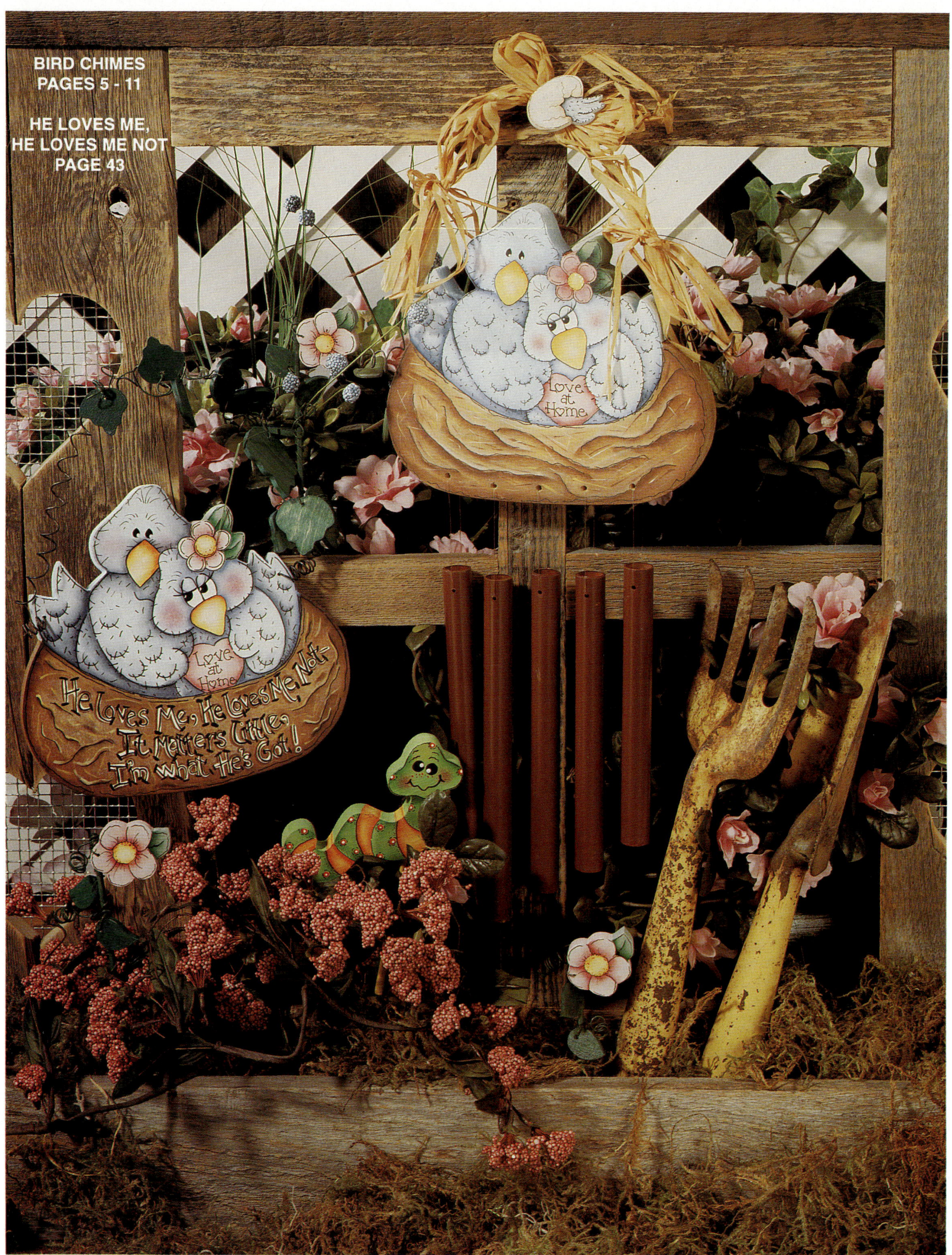
BIRD CHIMES
PAGES 5 - 11

HE LOVES ME,
HE LOVES ME NOT
PAGE 43

Love
at
Home

Love
at
Home

He Loves Me, He Loves Me Not~
It Matters Little,
I'm what He's Got!

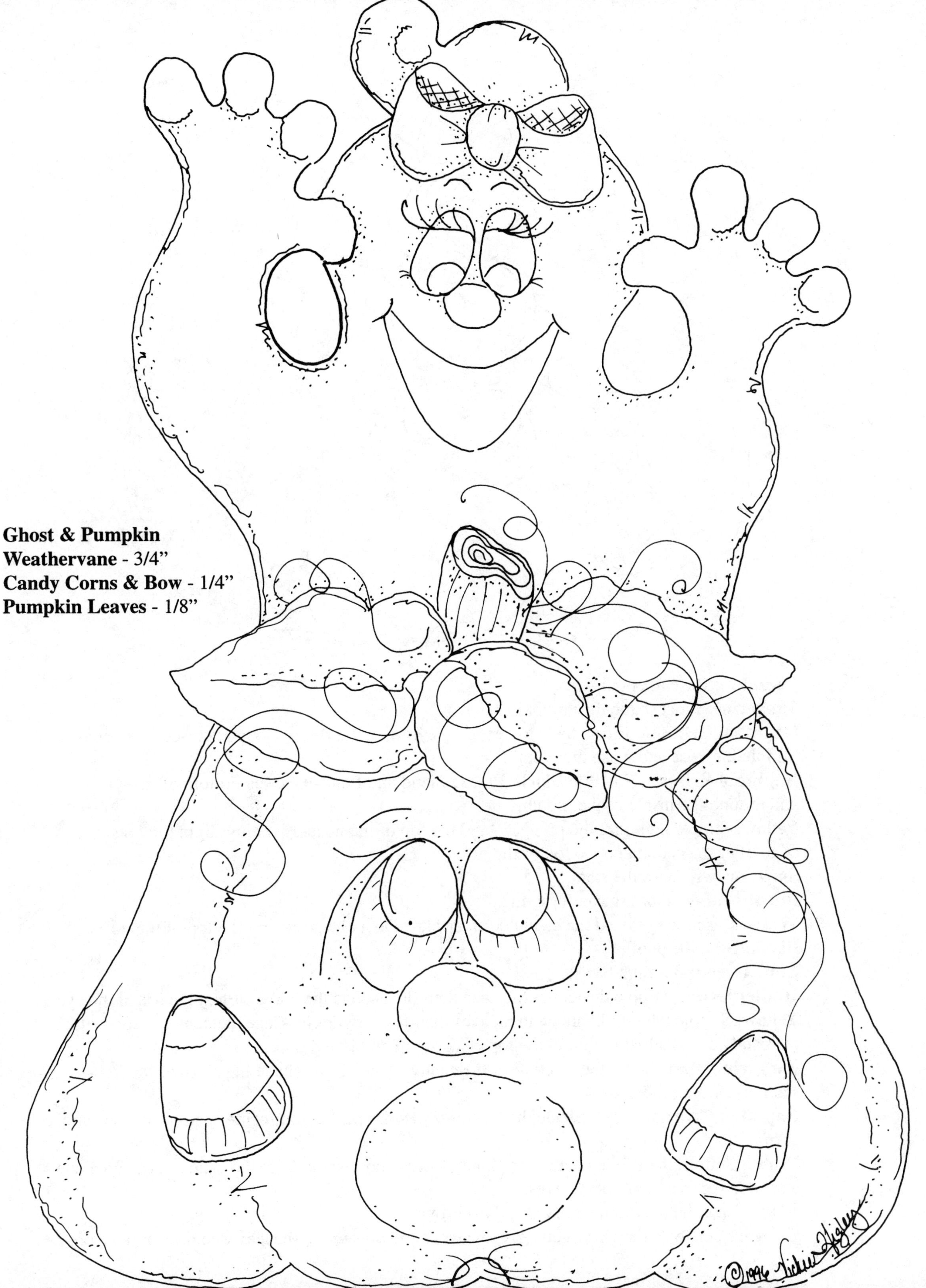

Ghost & Pumpkin
Weathervane - 3/4"
Candy Corns & Bow - 1/4"
Pumpkin Leaves - 1/8"

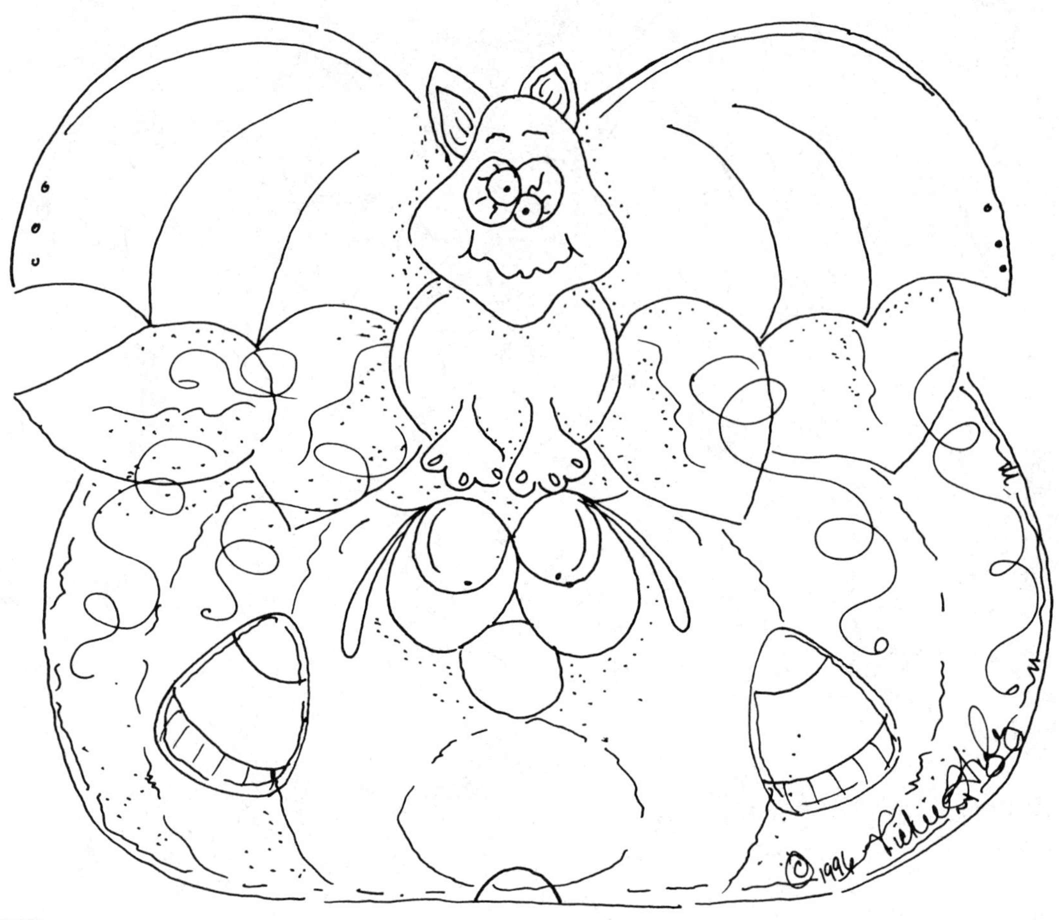

PUMPKINS

Pumpkin: Base the pumpkins.

Tangerine: Float shade the pumpkin.

Naphthol Crimson: Float shade to deepen the **Tangerine** float. Do the "crescent" strokes. Stipple the nose and wash the mouth.

Naphthol Crimson + a little Black: Palette blend and float shade the bottom of the nose and around the inside of the mouth.

Yellow: Stipple highlight the pumpkin and the top of the nose. Float highlight the outside edge of each section and the top of the nose.

Spice Brown: Base the stem.

Burnt Umber: Float shade the stem.

White: Base the eyes and the candy corn cheeks. Do a one stroke on the top of the nose.

Black: Base the pupils.

Lime Green: Base the leaves.

Hunter Green: Stipple the leaves to shade then float shade the leaves. Float the iris of the eye.

Yellow: Stipple the highlights on the leaves then float highlight. Base the center section of the candy corns. Float highlight the top of the stem and line the stem.

Tangerine: Base the bottom section of the candy corns. Float shade the sides of the Yellow sections of the candy corns.

Naphthol Crimson: Float Shade the bottom and sides of the **Tangerine** sections of the candy corns.

White: Start in the White area of the Candy Corns and reverse float the candy corn. Do a one stroke in the eyes and dot the eyes.

Black: Line the mouth, nose, eyes and eyebrows

Use your pen to do the vines, squiggly line work and dots under the leaves and around the nose.

BATS and SPIDER

Black: Base the Bats and Spider
White: Base the eyes, float highlight the top of the wings and the wing sections, the face and the feet.
Naphthol Crimson: Dot the eyes and wash inside the ears. Stipple the cheeks. Pull the tiny veins in the eyes.
White: Dot the center of the eyes. Line the mouth, wings and body, eyebrows and little strokes in the ears.
Egg Plant + White (1:4): On the bat, line the top of the wings, sides of the body and do tiny one strokes for the toes.
Blue Danube & White: 1:5 Float shade behind the spider's web.

SPIDER'S BOOTS

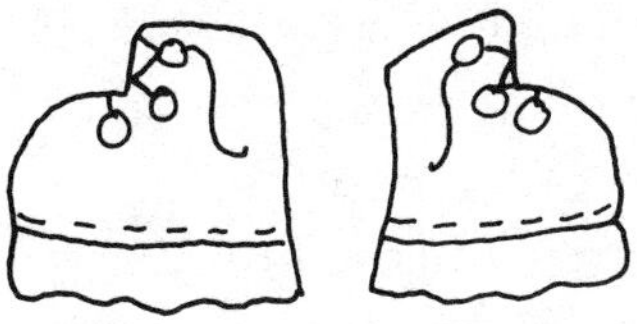

Spice Brown: Wash the soles.
Burnt Umber: Float shade the soles.
Tangerine: Wash the boots.
Naphthol Crimson: Float shade the boots.
Yellow: Float highlight the toe and across the eyelet area.
Naphthol Crimson: Dot the eyelets.
Use your pen to do the laces, outline the eyelets and the stitching.

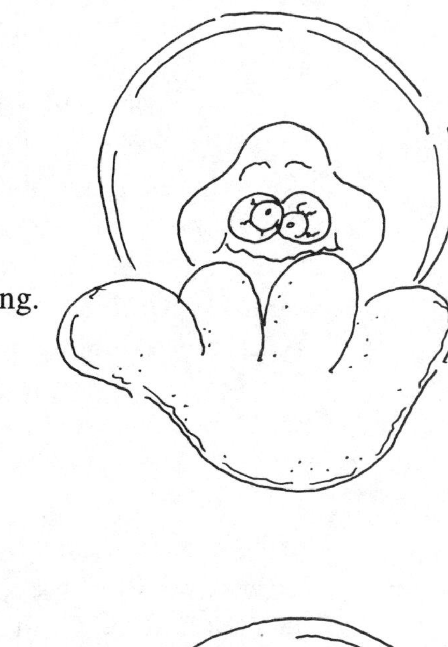

**Large Ghost for bottom of
Chime & Weathervane - 3/4"**

**Witch's hand w/ Spider - 1/2"
Spider Boots - 1/8"**

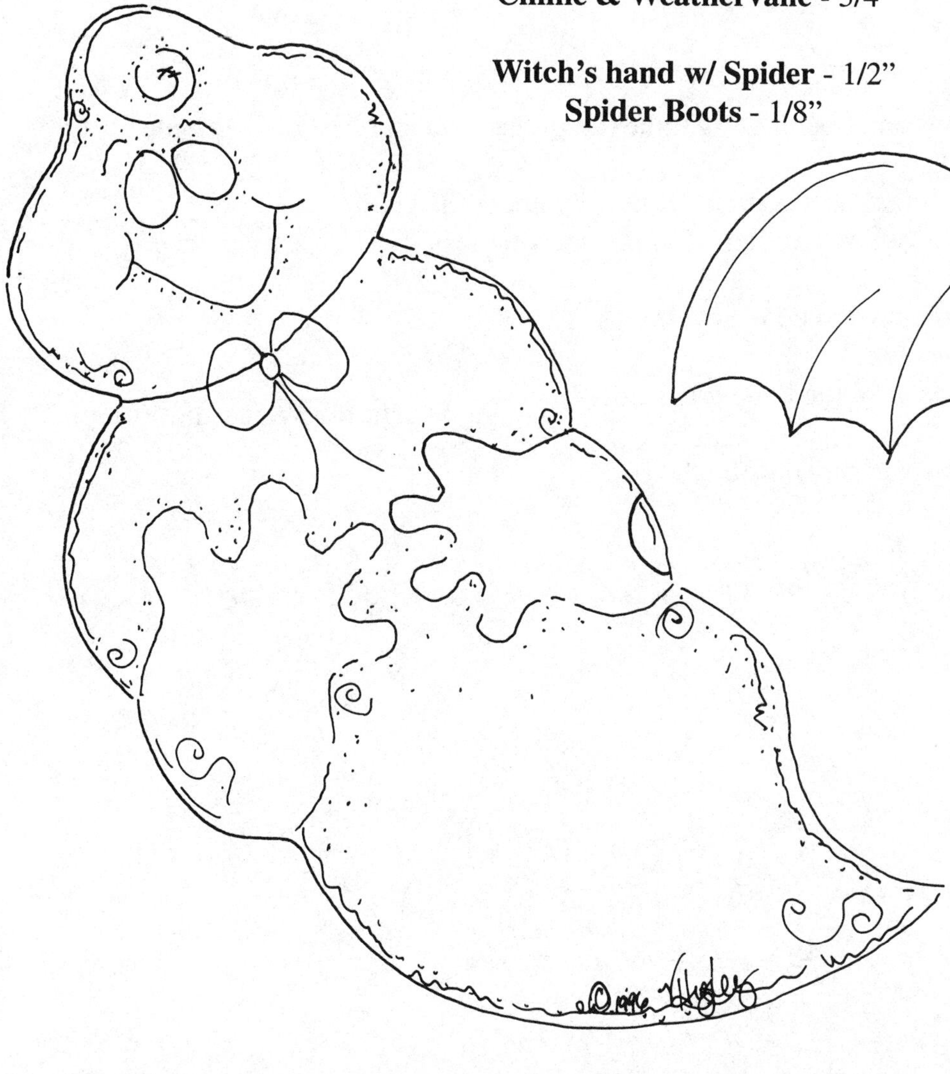

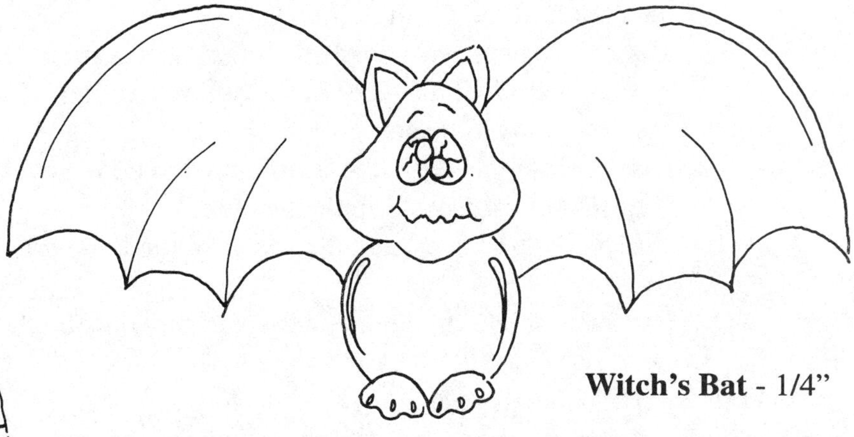

Witch's Bat - 1/4"

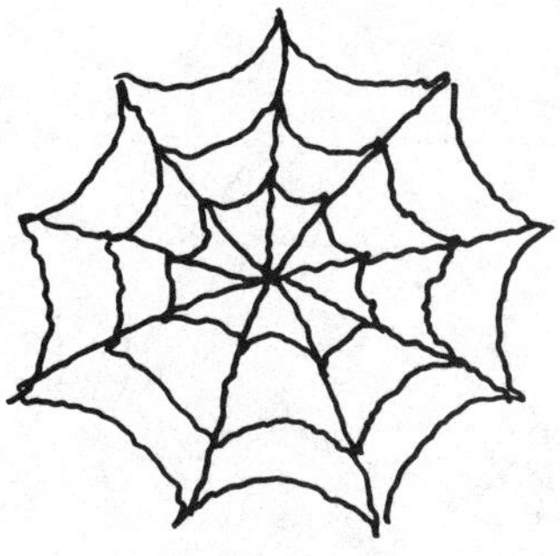

WITCHES POT

White: Base the top bubbles that stick above the pot.
Lime Green: Base the goo inside the pot. Wash the edges of the top white bubbles.
Spice Brown: Wash the spoon handle.
Black: Base the pot.
Hunter Green: Float shade the green goo.
Burnt Umber: Float shade the sides and bottom of the spoon.
Light Ivory: Float highlight the top of the spoon.
Blue Danube: Float shade and float highlight the pot. Float under the rim on the pot and on the very top edge of the rim as it meets the goo.
Egg Plant + White: Don't mix it completely. Have darks and lights in the paint. Use your liner or a small round and do the lettering.
White: Wash all the rest of the bubbles.
Make sure each layer of paint in the following steps is completely dry before proceeding to the next step. Keep all of the floats very sheer. Have extra water in your brush and a little paint. You want the pot to show through.
Lime Green: Float around the edges of all the bubbles.
Hunter Green: Float the bottoms of some bubbles.
Lime Green: Float the bottoms of some bubbles.
White: Float highlight the tops of some of the bubbles.
Black: Line the spoon around the inside edge of the pot skipping the areas where there are bubbles.

WORM

Lime Green: Base the green areas.
Yellow: Base the orange sections and float highlight the top of the head and the chin. Stipple the center of the green sections.
Hunter Green: Float shade the green sections. Float heavily under the chin.
Tangerine: Float the sides of the **Yellow** sections. Do the dots on the body. Use a stylus to do the tiny dots on the nose.
Black: Base the eyes, line the mouth and do the eyebrows.
Naphthol Crimson: Stipple the cheeks.
White: Dot the eyes, and the center of the large orange dots.

Use your pen to do the line work and tiny dots on the body.

THE BASE

Crocus: Base the base and the dowel for the worm.

Worm for Welcome Witch - 1/2"

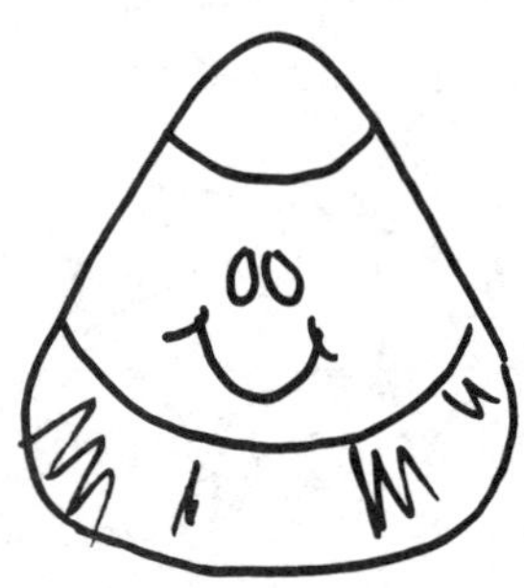

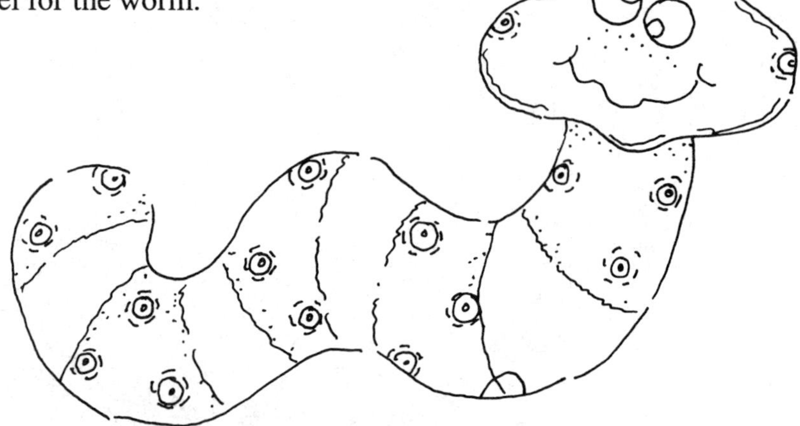

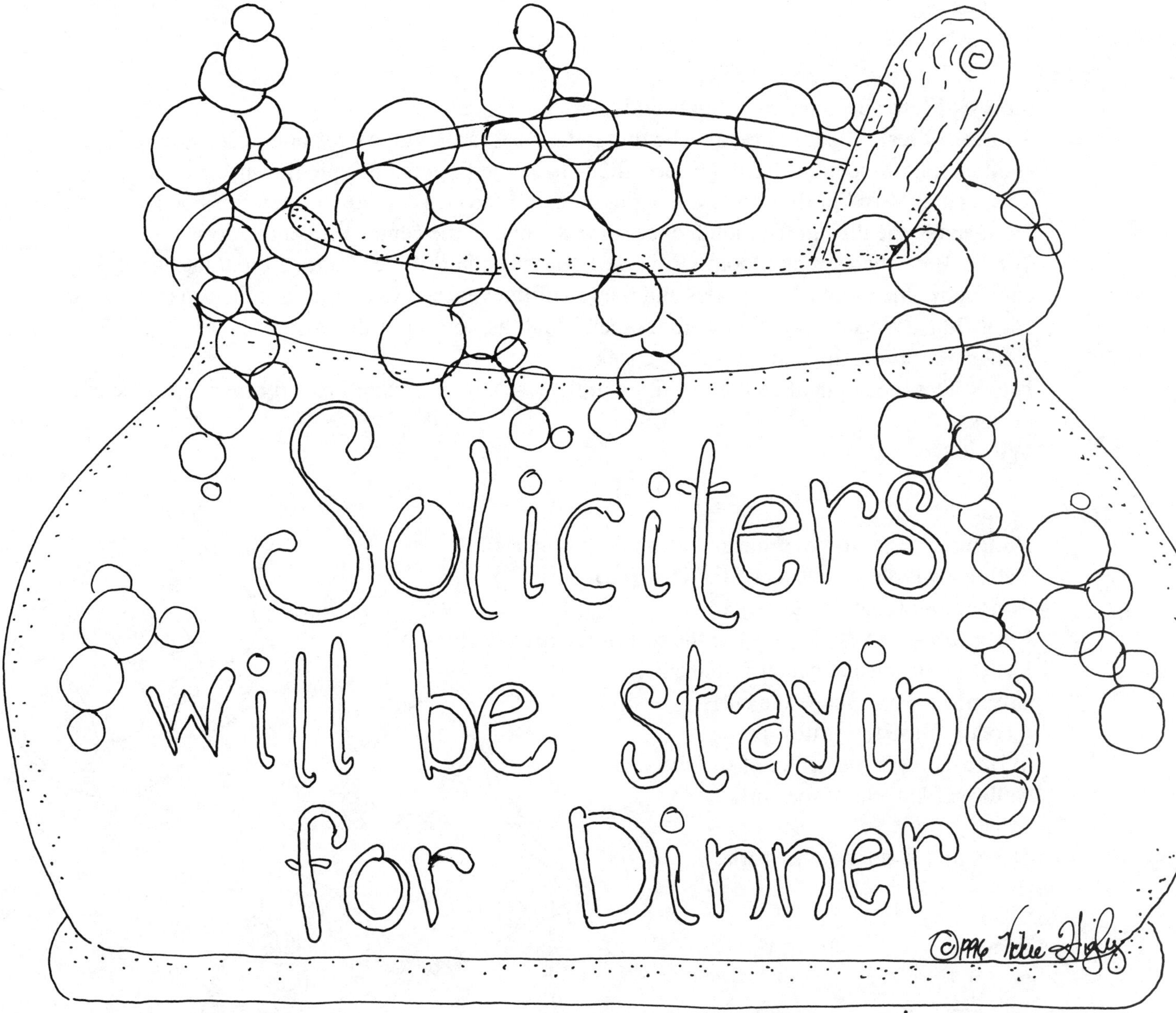

Welcome Witch's Pot - 3/4"
Witch's Star for wand - 1/2"

STAR

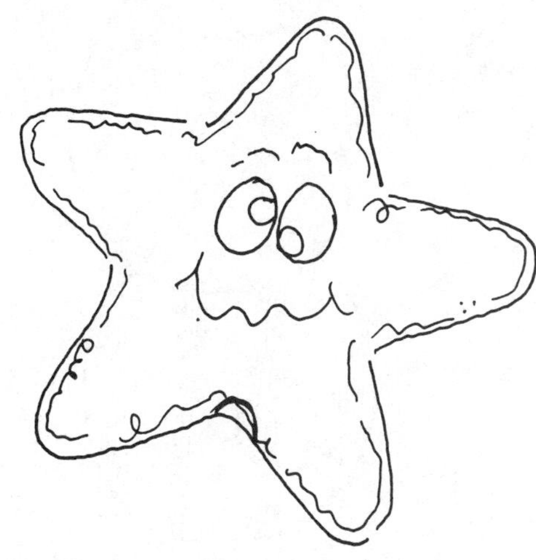

Yellow: Base the star.
Golden Brown: Float shade some of the edges of the star.
White: Stipple the center of the star.
Black: Base the eyes, line the mouth and eyebrows.
White: Dot the eyes.
Naphthol Crimson: Stipple the cheeks.
Pumpkin: Base the wand.
Tangerine: Stipple the wand here and there.

Use your pen to do the squiggly lines around the star.

WITCH

Santa's Flesh: Base the face hands and legs.
Medium Flesh: Float shade the face under the curls, around the eyes and nose, sides of the eyelids, top of the mouth and the ears float shade the fingers. Stipple the shading on the legs.
Tangerine: Very lightly stipple a few places under the curls and under her dress on her legs. Float shade the dips in the mouth except for the one in the center. Wash the nose.
White: Base the eyes and tooth. Reverse float the center of the eyelids. Float highlight the ears, under the mouth, her fingers and the top of the knees. Float highlight the top of the nose.
Naphthol Crimson: Stipple the cheeks and float the bottom of the nose.
Tangerine: Float the bottom for the cheeks
Black: Dot the pupils, line the facial features. Use a liner or small round brush to do the eye lashes.
White: Dot the iris.

HAIR

Pumpkin: Base some of the curls (the darkest curls).
Yellow: Stipple the center of the **Pumpkin** curls.
Tangerine: Float Shade the curls.
Pumpkin + White (1:4): Base the rest of the orange curls.
Crocus: Stipple the center of the curls.
Pumpkin: Float shade the curls.
Crocus: Base the yellow curls.
White: Stipple the center of the curls.
Yellow: Float shade the curls.

Use a pen to do the line work

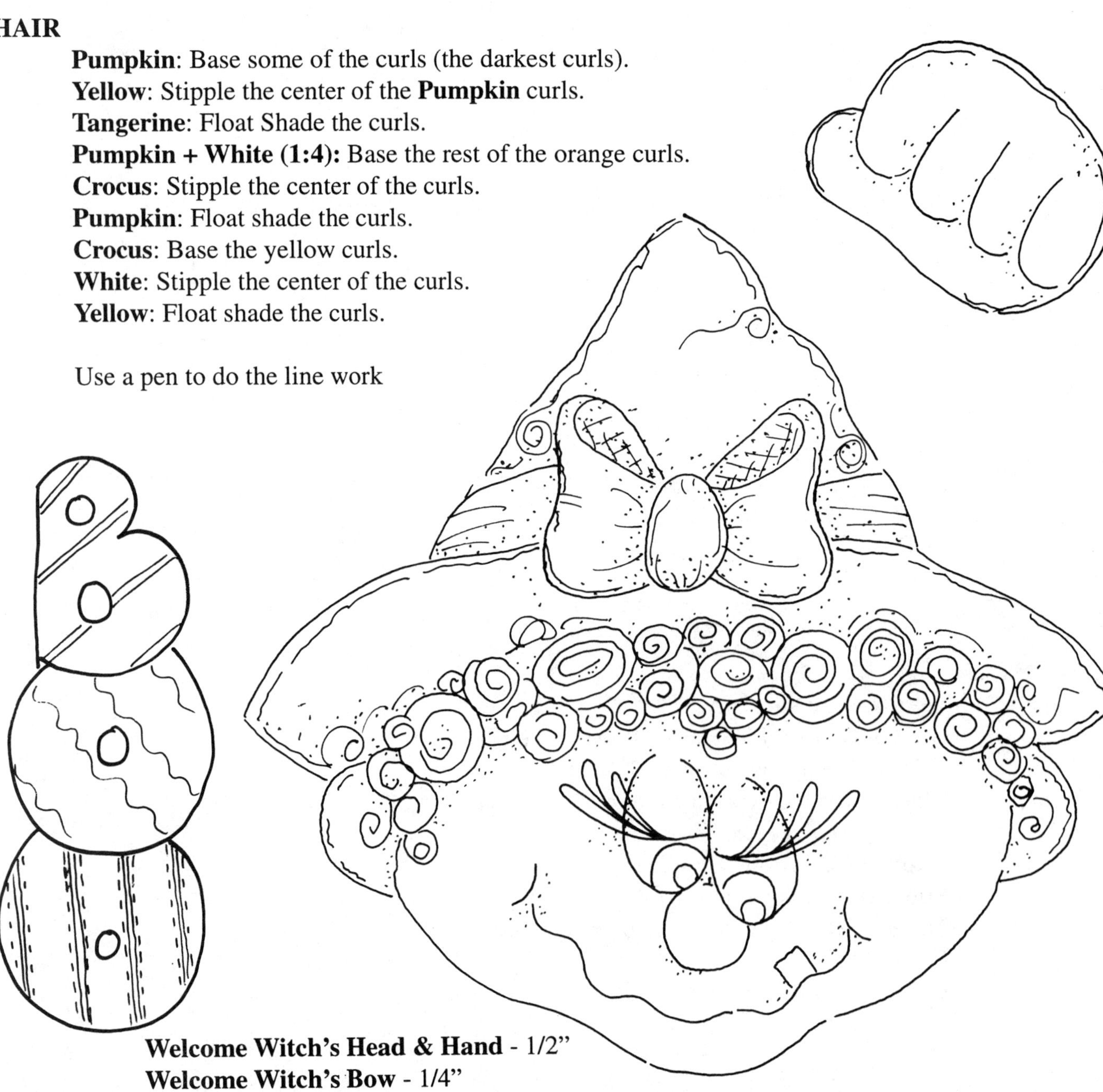

Welcome Witch's Head & Hand - 1/2"
Welcome Witch's Bow - 1/4"

WELCOME ASSEMBLY

Bend the chenille stems into the shape of the letter "Z". Hot Glue the stems to the spiders boots. Check for placement and hot glue the legs to the back of the spiders body. Use wood glue to attach the pieces to the body. Attach the screw eyes to the base and pot. Fasten the base to the pot with 12" of wire for each side. Twist to secure. Curl the ends of the wire and trim. Tie a bow with the orange raffia and hot glue in place on the base. Curl 7" of wire for the bat and attach the bat to the hat.

WIND CHIME ASSEMBLY

Cut the pipes according to the General Directions. I sprayed he pipes with several light layers of Krylon Black Spray. Attach the screw eyes. Cut and curl 24" of wire around the end of a large brush and thread through the screw eyes. Bend the ends around and cut off any extra wire. Attach a screw eye to the bottom center of the base, to the top and bottom of the small ghost and the top of the large ghost. Attach all together with fishing line. Tie 3 raffia bows and hot glue or wire in place.

WEATHERVANE ASSEMBLY

Make 4 Raffia Bows each with 1 yd of black ribbon and tie onto the weathervane dowels. Wood glue the cheeks and bow on.

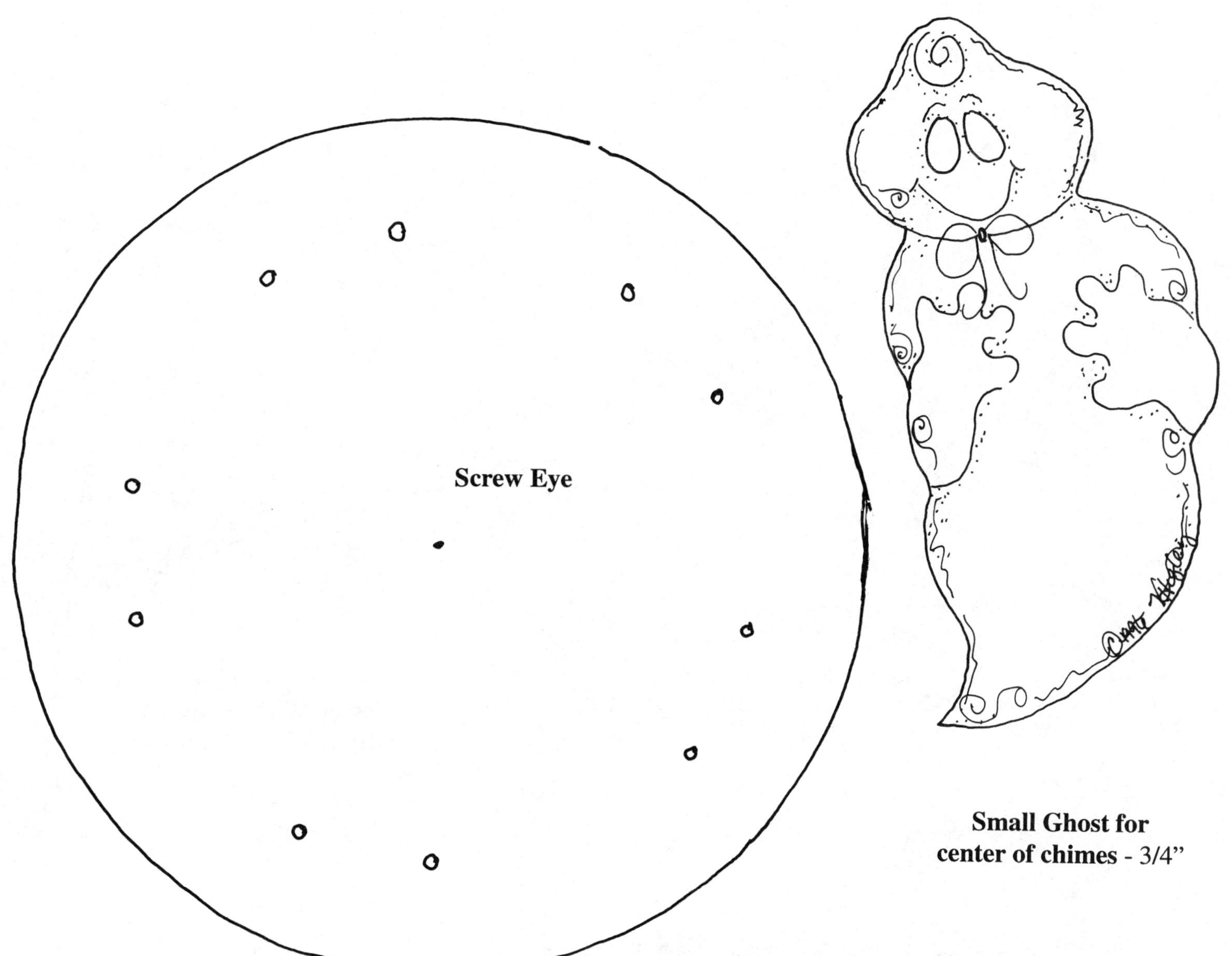

**Small Ghost for
center of chimes - 3/4"**

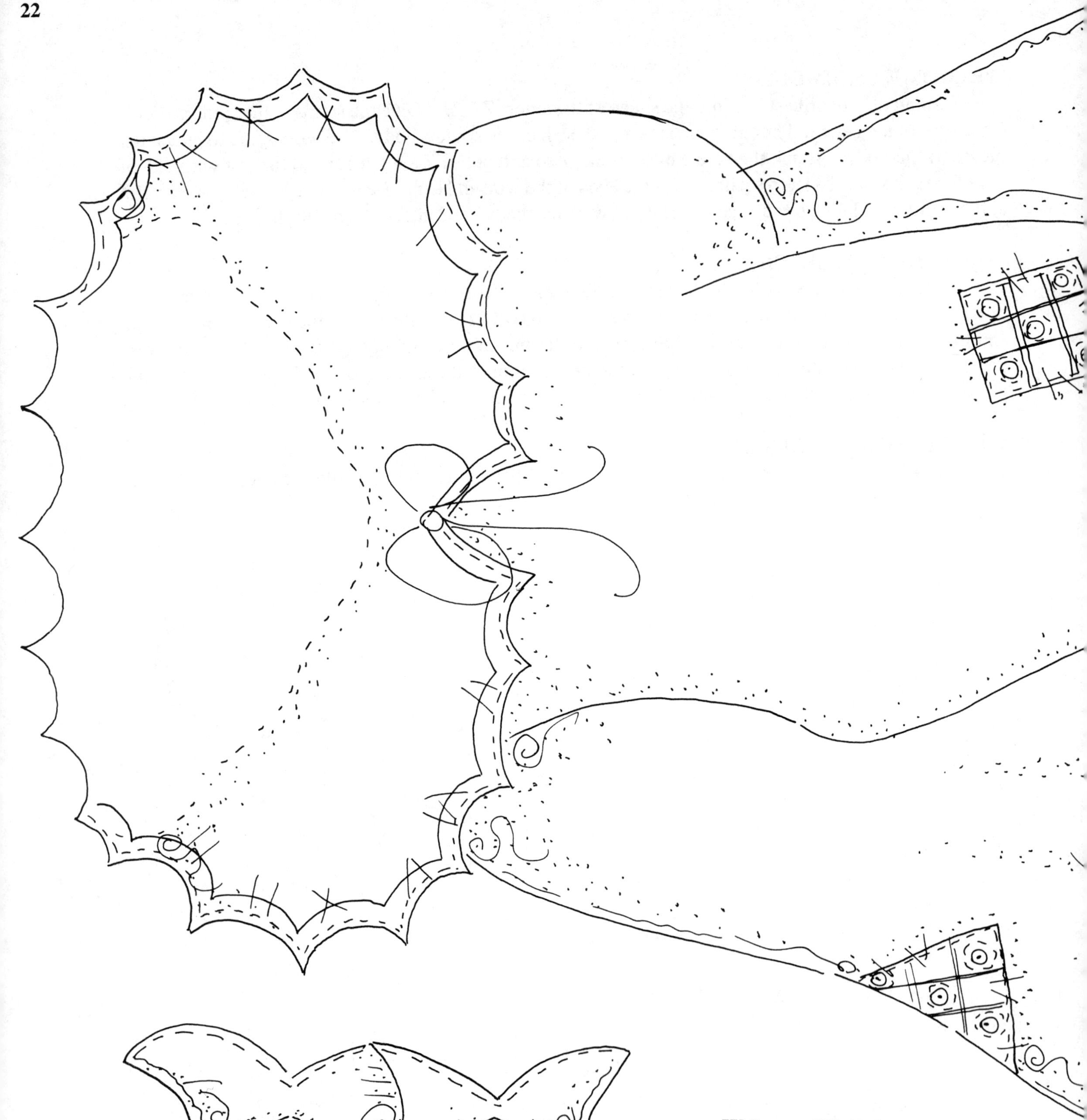

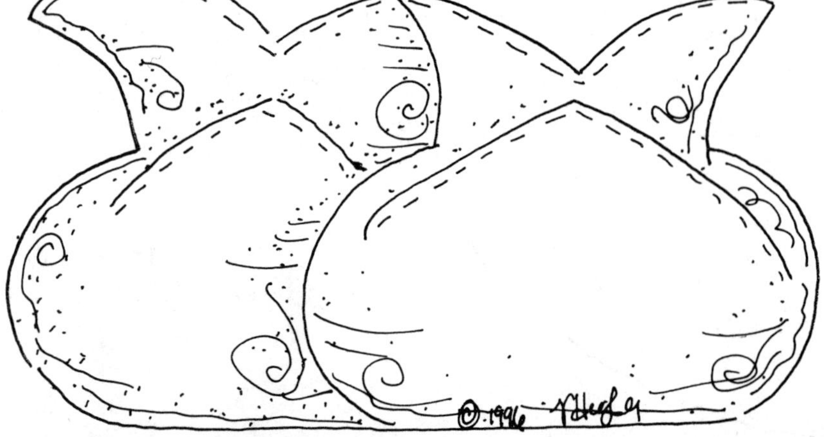

Welcome Witch Body - 3/4"
Welcome Witch Boots - 1/2"

© 1996

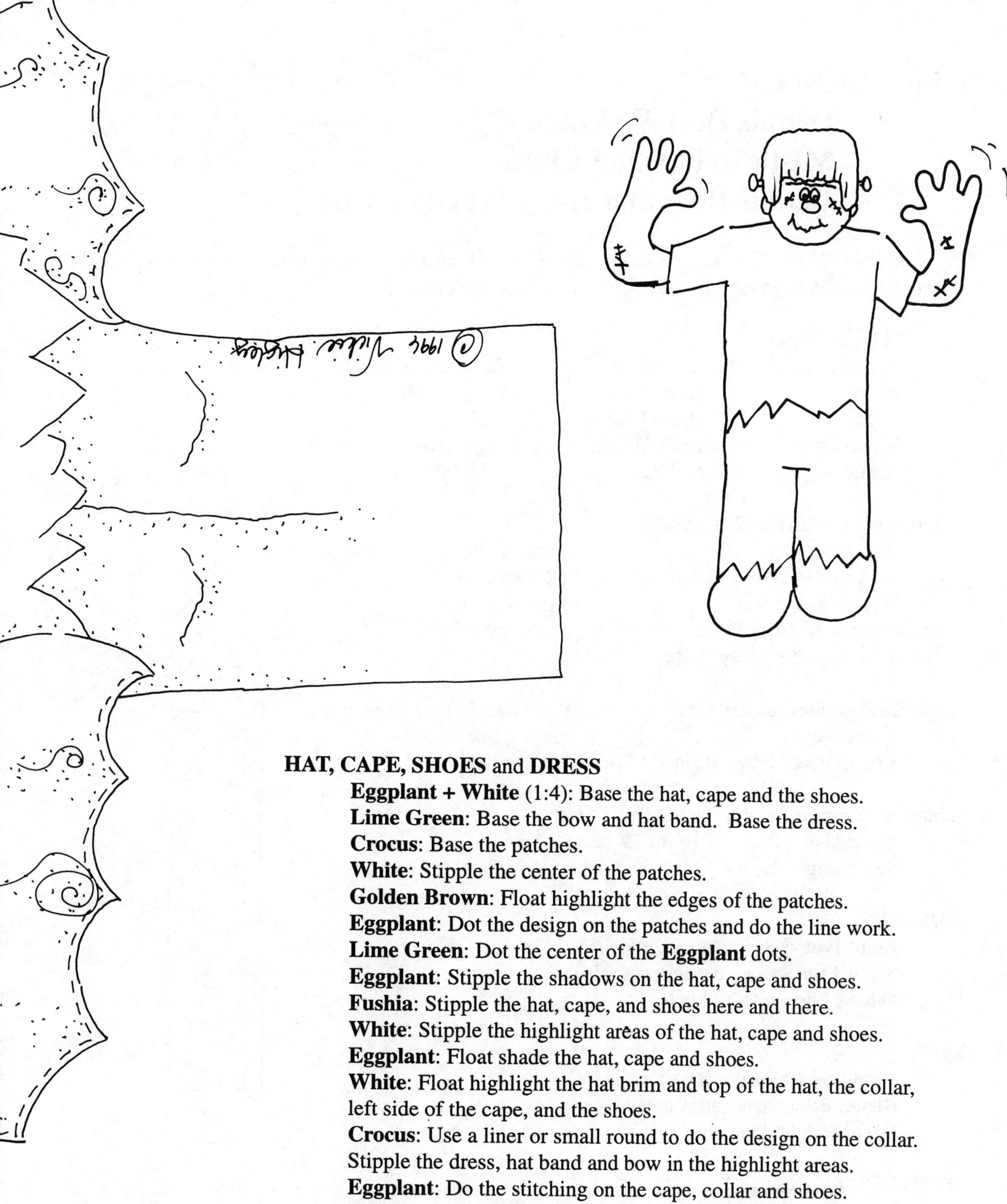

HAT, CAPE, SHOES and DRESS

    Eggplant + White (1:4): Base the hat, cape and the shoes.
    Lime Green: Base the bow and hat band. Base the dress.
    Crocus: Base the patches.
    White: Stipple the center of the patches.
    Golden Brown: Float highlight the edges of the patches.
    Eggplant: Dot the design on the patches and do the line work.
    Lime Green: Dot the center of the **Eggplant** dots.
    Eggplant: Stipple the shadows on the hat, cape and shoes.
    Fushia: Stipple the hat, cape, and shoes here and there.
    White: Stipple the highlight areas of the hat, cape and shoes.
    Eggplant: Float shade the hat, cape and shoes.
    White: Float highlight the hat brim and top of the hat, the collar, left side of the cape, and the shoes.
    Crocus: Use a liner or small round to do the design on the collar. Stipple the dress, hat band and bow in the highlight areas.
    Eggplant: Do the stitching on the cape, collar and shoes.
    Hunter Green: Stipple the shading on the dress, hat band and bow and then Float Shade those areas.
Use your pen to do the outlining, pepper dots, and squiggles.
Varnish the wood pieces with Krylon Matte Spray Finish

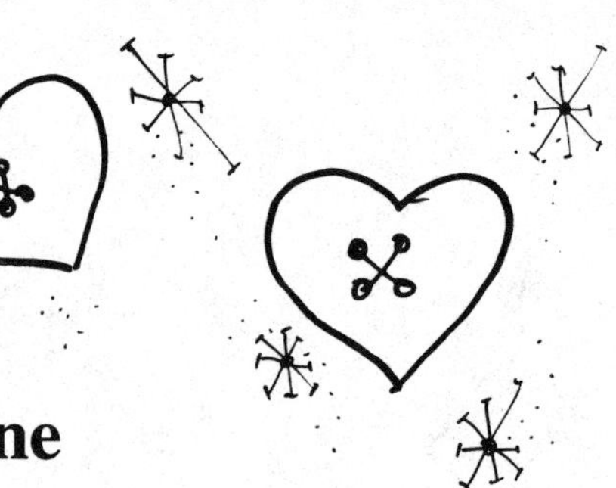

Painting directions for:

Dennis Deer Welcome
MistleToad Wind Chime
Dennis Deer and Holly Weather Vane

DENNIS DEER looks a bit dazed, doesn't he. It must be all those kisses! I hope you have a "Deer" Christmas at your house and watch out for that MistleToad!

PALETTE (by Delta)

Naphthol Crimson	Tangerine	Gleams 14K Gold	Barn Red
Black	Lime Green	Hunter Green	Crocus
Straw	Burnt Umber	Yellow	White
Hippo Grey	Spice Brown	Light Ivory	Spice Tan
Maple Sugar	Old Parchment	Midnight	Sparkle Glaze

Additional Supplies for WELCOME:

Wood glue	4 yds of 1/4" Metallic Ribbon
1/2 yd of 1/16" red ribbon	16, 5 mm bells
3' of 19 gauge wire	4 screw eyes
Fantasy Snow by Delta	Sea sponge
Renaissance Foil By Delta	

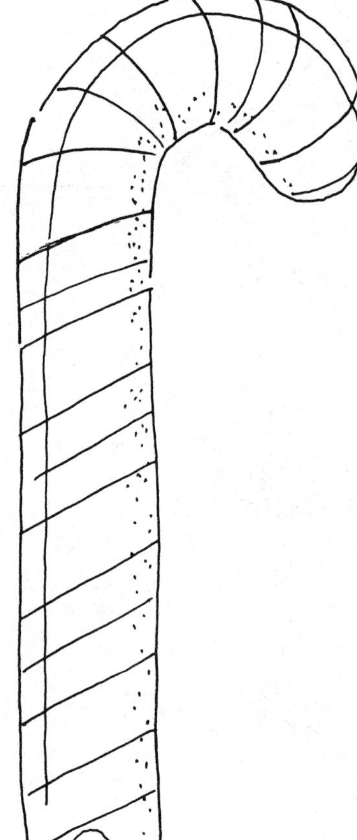

Additional Supplies for CHIMES:

	Pipes (see General Directions)
2 Screw eyes	Fishing line
Krylon Black Spray Paint	Wood glue

Additional Supplies for the WEATHER VANE:

Wood glue	10" of 19 gauge wire
Sea Sponge	1/4" picot ribbon, 4 yards of red and green

ANTLERS

Light Ivory: Basecoat the antlers.
Spice Tan: Sponge the antlers to shade.
White: Sponge to highlight.

LIPS

Naphthol Crimson: Base the lips.
Black: Base the negative areas.
Barn Red: Outline the lips.

DEER BODY

Spice Tan: Basecoat the body and face.
Maple Sugar: Sponge the entire body and face.
Old Parchment: Sponge the face and body in the highlight areas.
Spice Brown: Float shade the body and face.
Old Parchment: Float highlight the face and body.

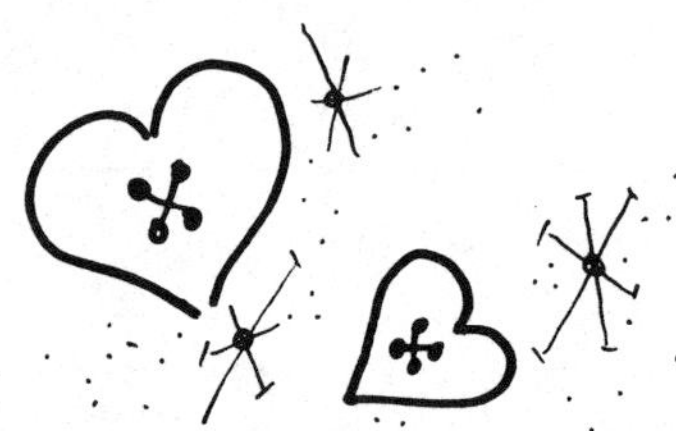

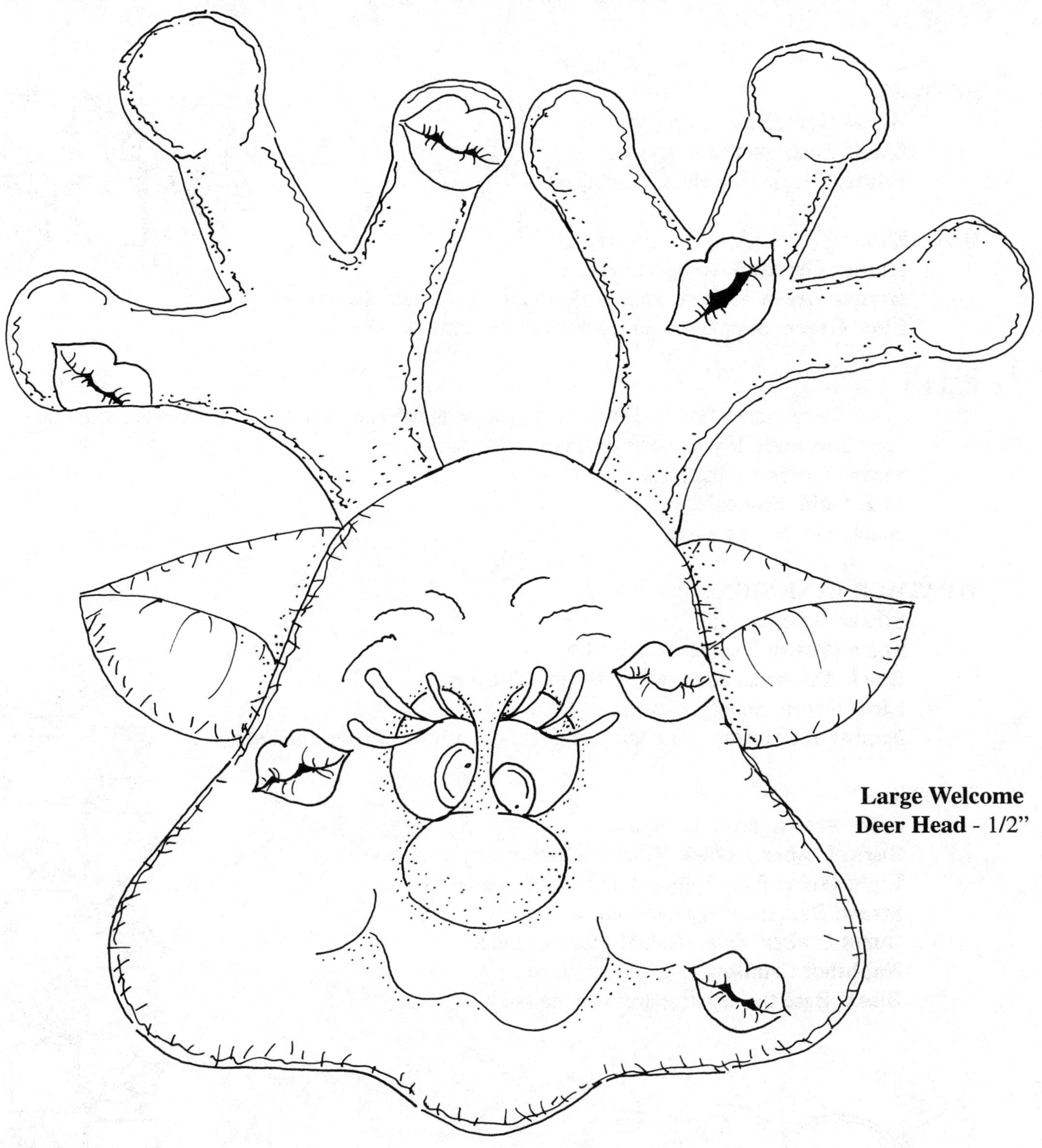

FACE

Barn Red: Wash inside of ears and stipple the cheeks.

Naphthol Crimson: Base the nose.

Barn Red + a little **Black**: Stipple the lower half of the nose then float shade.

Tangerine: Stipple the top half of the nose and then float highlight.

White: Base the eyes.

Black: Base the pupils.

White: Float the highlight in the eyes and dot the eyes. Reverse float the center of the eyelids.

Black: Outline the mouth, nose, eyes and eyebrows. I used a Loew Cornell #2 round to do the eyelashes.

Use your pen to do the squiggly outlining.

HOOVES

Hippo Grey: Base the hooves.
Black: Float shade the hooves.
White: Stipple the center of the hooves.

HARNESS

Hunter Green: Base the harness.
Hunter Green + Black: Palette blend and float shade the harness.
Lime Green: Stipple the center areas of the harness.

BELLS

I used Renaissance Foil by Delta. This process is fun and easy to do. Follow the manufactures directions. If you prefer, paint on the bells:
Straw: Undercoat the bells.
14 K Gold: Base the bells.
Black: Do the line work.

WEATHER VANE SIGN

Straw: Base the sign.
Spice Brown: Float shade the edges.
Black: Do the lettering with a #1 Jackie's Liner.
Lime Green: Squiggly lines.
Naphthol Crimson: Base the hearts and use a stylus to the small dots.

BOOTS

Spice Brown: Base the boots.
Burnt Umber + Black: Float shade and stipple the boots.
Light Ivory: Float highlight and stipple the boots.
Straw: Base the tongue, eyelets, and soles.
Burnt Umber: Float shade the tongue and soles.
Naphthol Crimson: Line the shoelace.
Black: Base the negative areas on the soles.

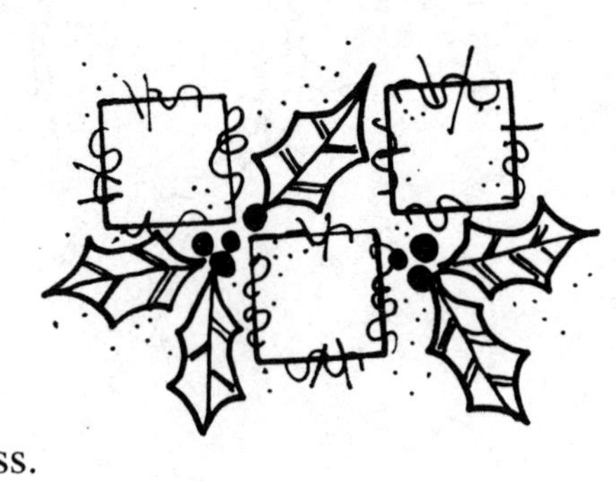

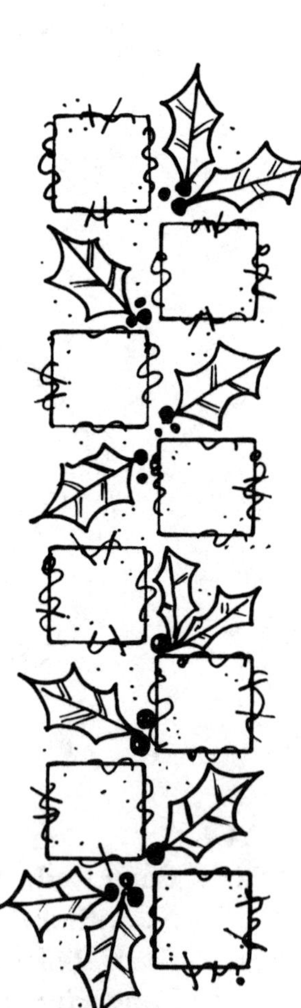

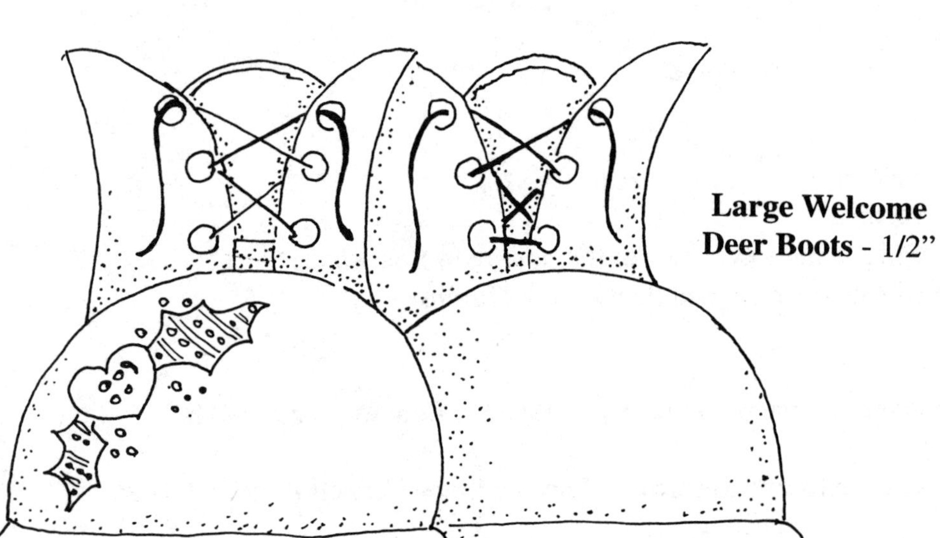

Large Welcome Deer Boots - 1/2"

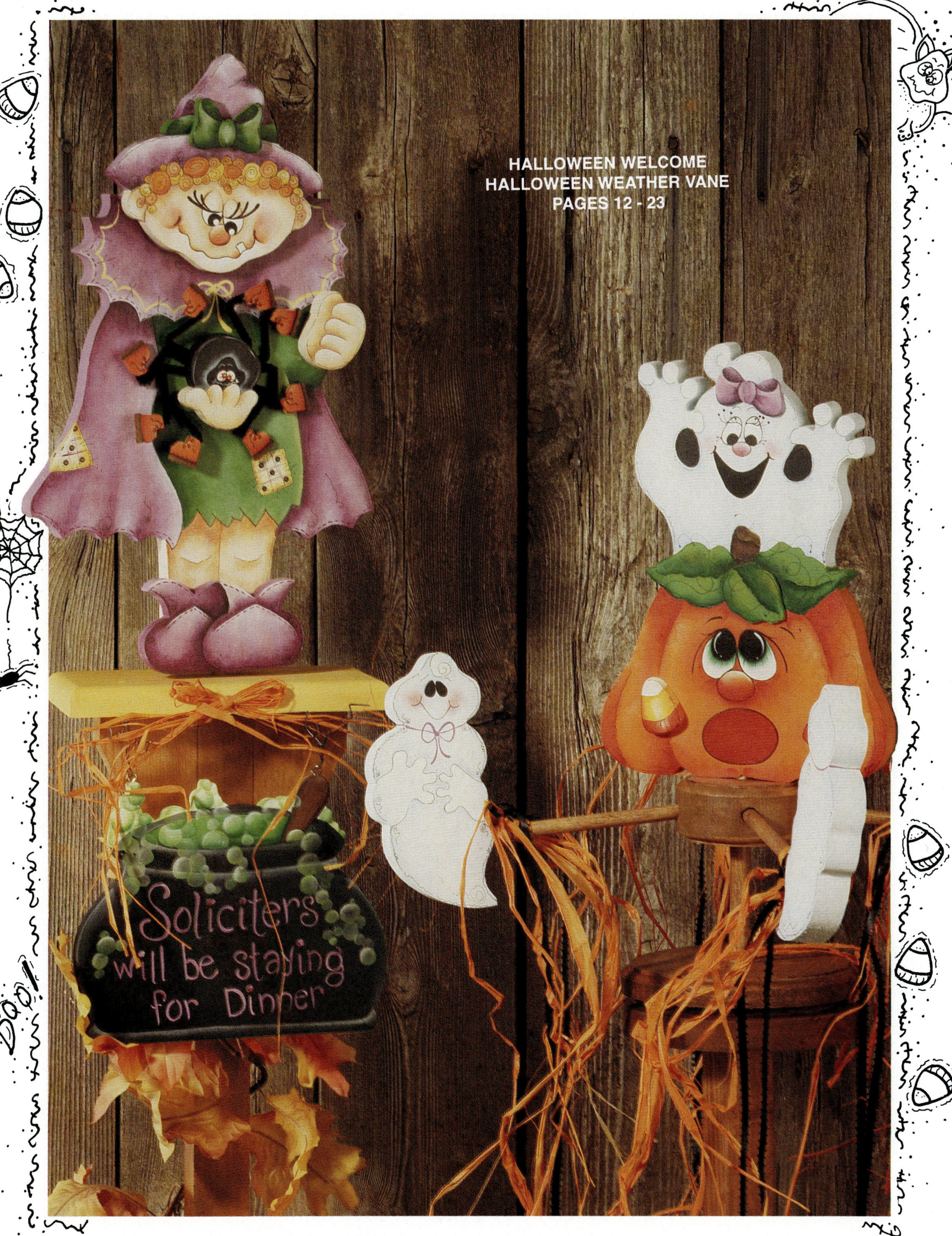
HALLOWEEN WELCOME
HALLOWEEN WEATHER VANE
PAGES 12 - 23
Soliciters
will be staying
for Dinner
BOO!

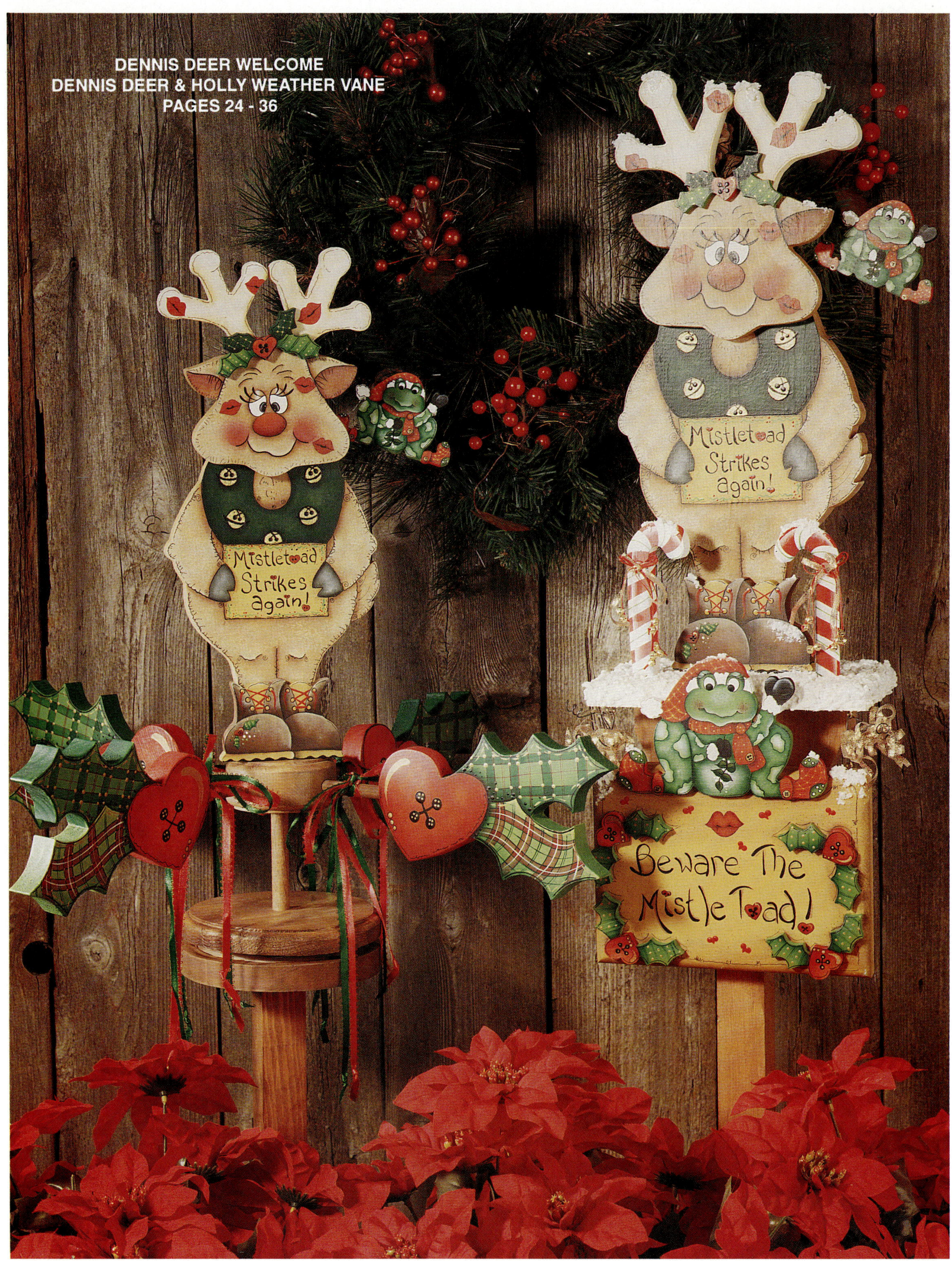

DENNIS DEER WELCOME
DENNIS DEER & HOLLY WEATHER VANE
PAGES 24 - 36
Mistletoad Strikes again!
Mistletoad Strikes again!
Beware The Mistle Toad!

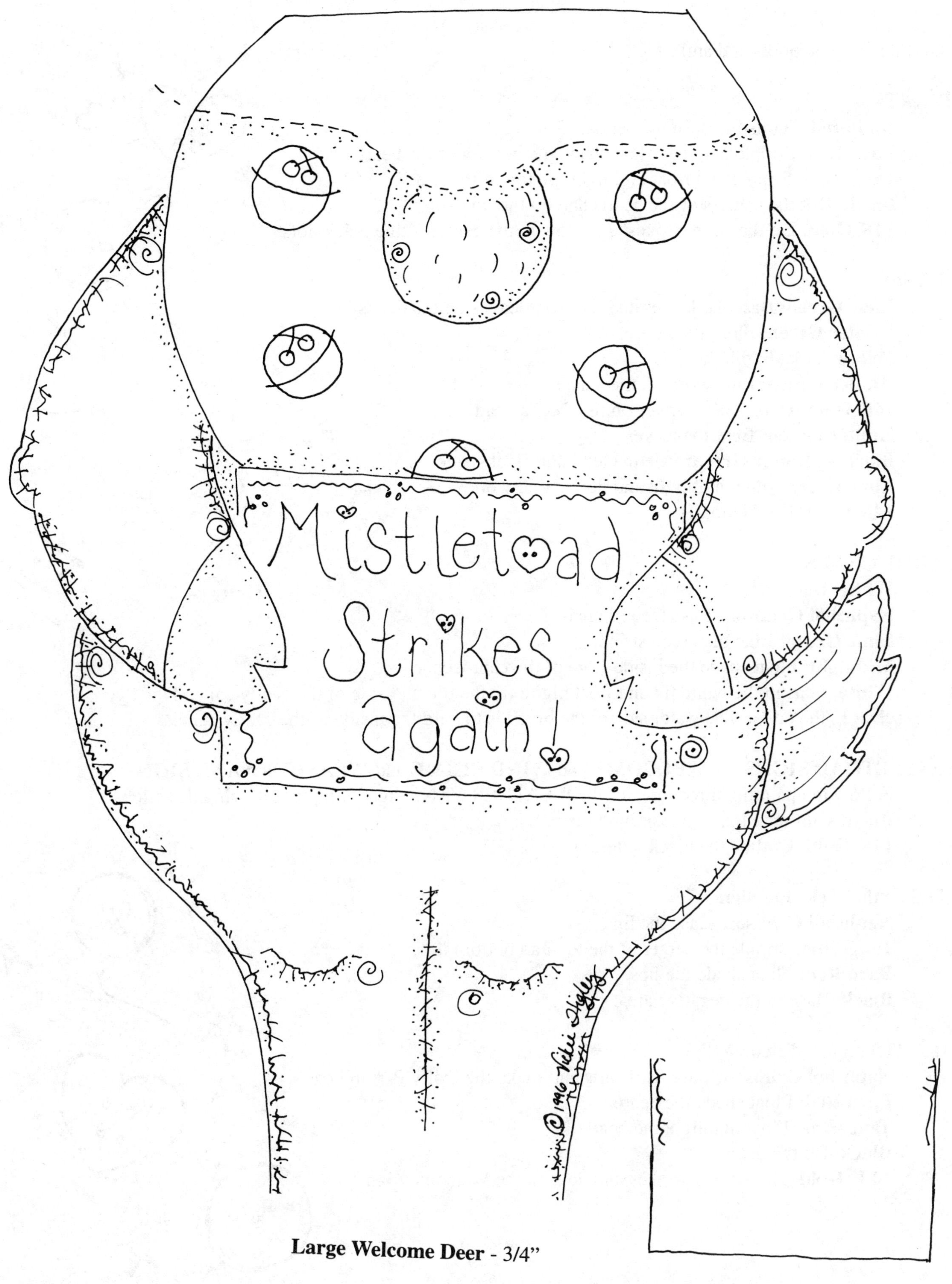

Large Welcome Deer - 3/4"

HOLLY for signs, boots and antlers

HEARTS

Naphthol Crimson: Base the hearts.
Barn Red: Stipple and then float shade the bottom of the heart.
Tangerine: Stipple and float highlight the top of the hearts.
Black: Dot the centers of the hearts and do the lines.
14K Gold: Do the "one strokes" and dots in the center of the black dots

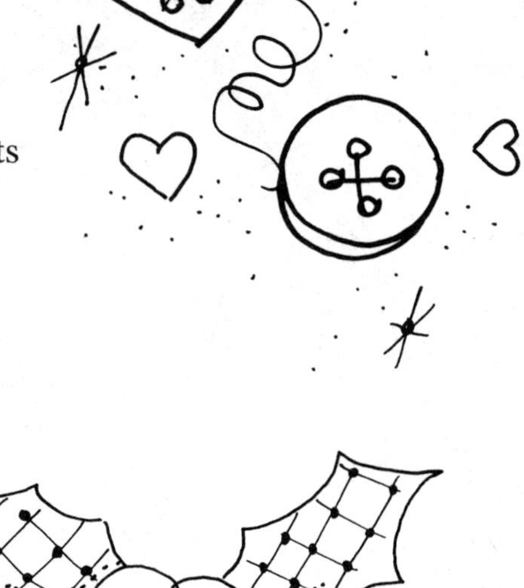

LEAVES

Lime Green: Base the leaves and the front leaves on the deer's head.
Hunter Green: Float shade.
Yellow: Float highlight.
Hunter Green: Line work on the leaves.
14K Gold: Dots. Back leaves on the Deer's head.
Hunter Green: Base the leaves.
Black + Hunter Green: Palette blend and float shade.
Lime Green: Float highlight and do the line work.
14K Gold: Do the dots.

CANDY CANES

White: Basecoat.
Naphthol Crimson: Base the red areas.
Lime Green: Line the green stripe.
Midnight: Float shade the inside edge of the candy cane
White: Start in the white tip and float highlight the top and side of the candy cane. Don't go clear to the edge. The water side of the brush is toward the inside of the candy cane.

Holly - 1/2"

MISTLETOAD SIGNS for WELCOME and WIND CHIME and WEATHER VANE SIGN

Follow the painting directions for the WEATHER VANE sign with the following directions:
Burnt Umber: Float shade around the holly.
14K Gold: Outline the black lettering.

LIPS on the Welcome Sign

Naphthol Crimson: Base the lips.
Tangerine: Stipple the center of the top and bottom lips.
Barn Red: Float shade the lips.
Black: Base in the negative area.

HEARTS on the Welcome Sign

Naphthol Crimson: Base the hearts and make the Dolly Parton hearts.
Barn Red: Float shade the hearts.
Tangerine: Float highlight the hearts.
Black: Do the dots.
14 K Gold: Do the one strokes and dots on the Welcome Sign.

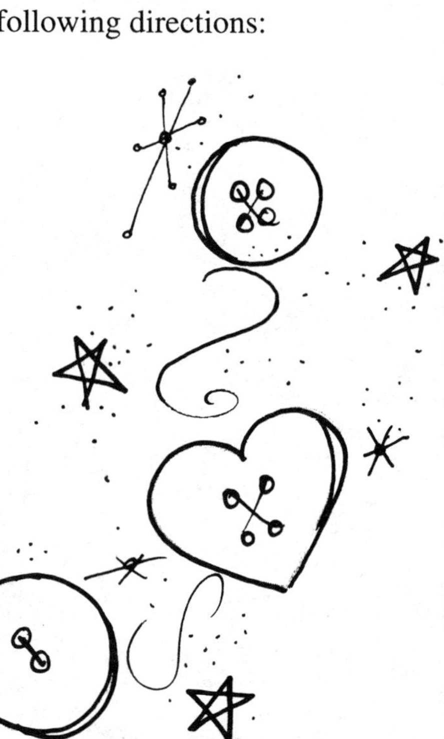

HOLLY LEAVES on the **Wind Chime** and **Welcome Sign**
> **Lime Green**: Base the leaves.
> **Hunter Green**: Float shade the leaves.
> **Crocus**: Float highlight.
> **Hunter Green**: Do the line work on the leaves.
> **14 K Gold**: Do the dots for the leaves on the Welcome Sign.
> **Sparkle Glaze**: the leaves.

> Use your pen to do the line work.

WEATHER VANE HOLLY HEARTS
> **Naphthol Crimson**: Base the hearts.
> **Barn Red**: Stipple the outside edges of the heart and then float shade.
> **Tangerine**: Stipple the center of the heart and then float shade.
> **Black**: Use the center of a large brush to make the dots.
> **14K Gold**: Do the one strokes and dot the center of the large dots.

**Large Welcome
Deer's Sign - 3/4"**

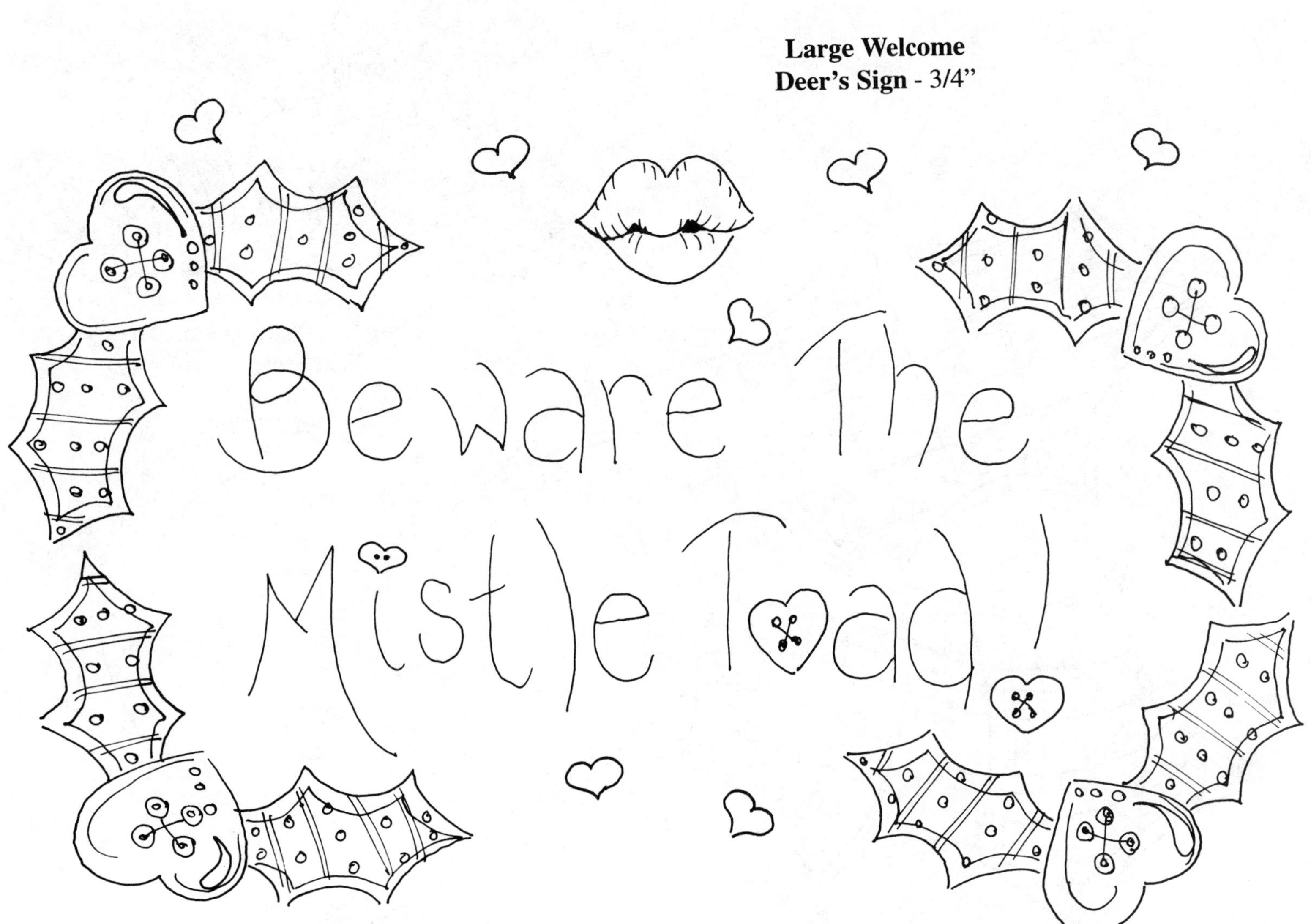

THE FRONT LEAF

Lime Green + Crocus (2:1): Base the front leaf.

Naphthol Crimson: Use a #8 flat to wash in the plaid. Make sure it is completely dry before going over it in the opposite direction.

Hunter Green: Outline the red plaid, do the double vertical stripes and 1 horizontal stripe across the bottom.

White: Do the stripes down the center of the red plaid.

14 K Gold: Dot the corners of the red plaid, stitch around the leaf.

THE BACK LEAF

Lime Green: Base the leaf.

Hunter Green: Use a #6 flat to wash in the plaid.

Naphthol Crimson: Outline the plaid and do the horizontal and double vertical stripes.

14K Gold: Dot the corners of the plaid and stitch around the leaf.

Hunter Green + Black: Float shade behind the heart and behind the front leaf.

Black: Dot the shadow areas on the leaves and outline the leaves.

Hunter Green: Wash the outside edges of the heart that is behind.

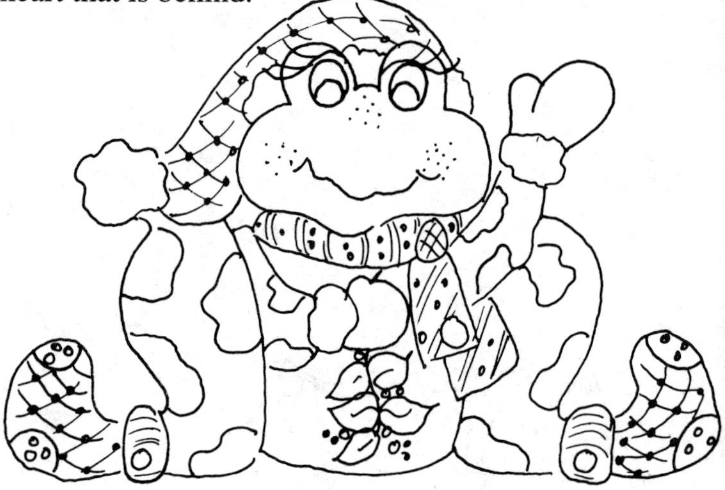

Frog for Weathervane Deer - 1/4”
Weathervane Holly - 3/4”

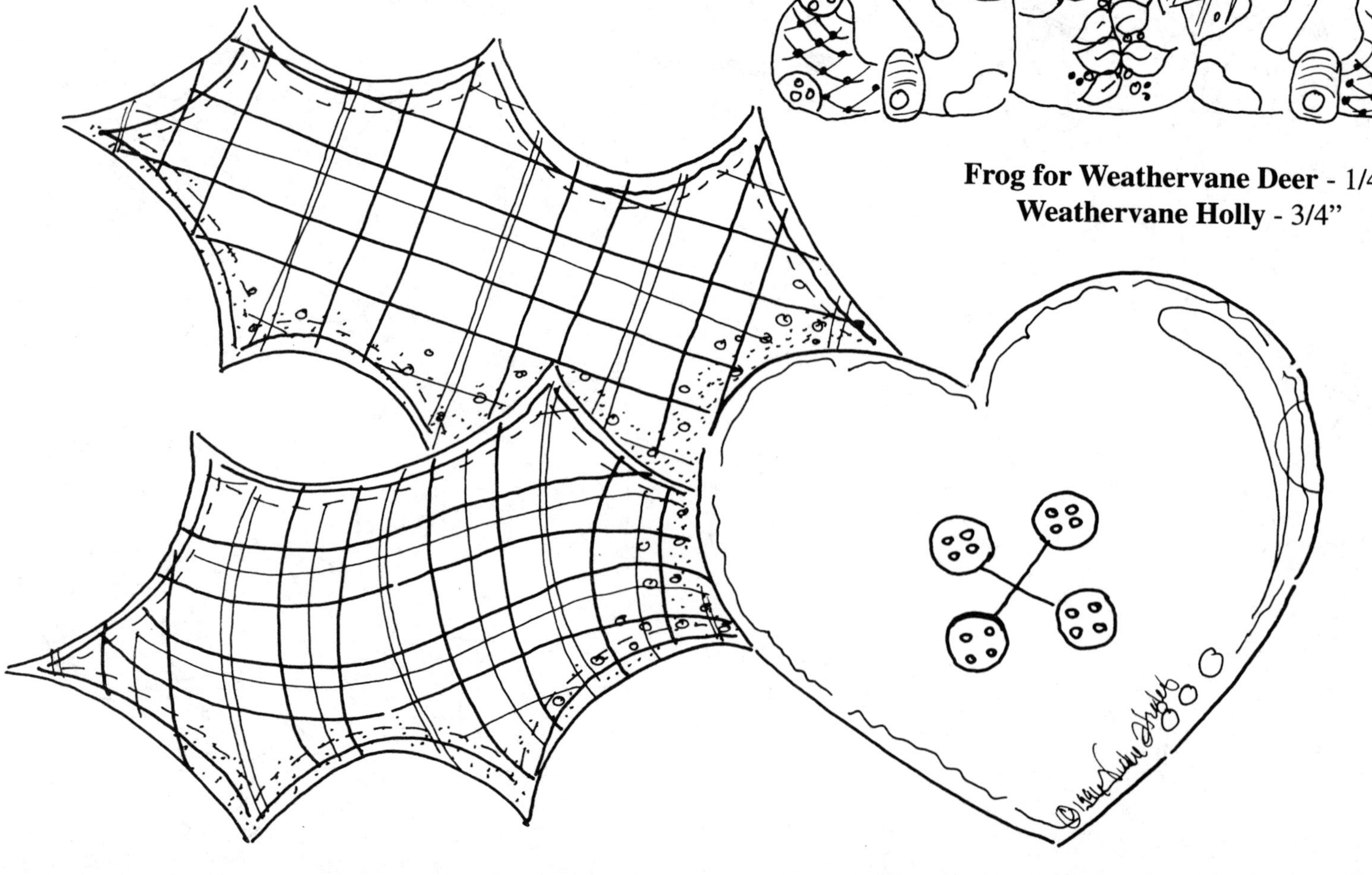

THE TOADS

Lime Green: Base the toad and the patches on the socks.
Lime Green + White: Base the patches on the body.
Black: Base the gloves.
White: Base the fur and the eyes. Stipple the body and lightly stipple the center of the patches and the nose. Float highlight the bottom of the chin and the top of the mouth and the gloves. Reverse float the center of the eyelids.
Naphthol Crimson: Base the scarf, hat and socks. Stipple the cheeks.
Hunter Green: Float shade the toad and around the patches. Base the leaves.
Black: Base the pupils and the negative area. Do the eyelashes and outline the eyes.
Lime Green: Float highlight the leaves.

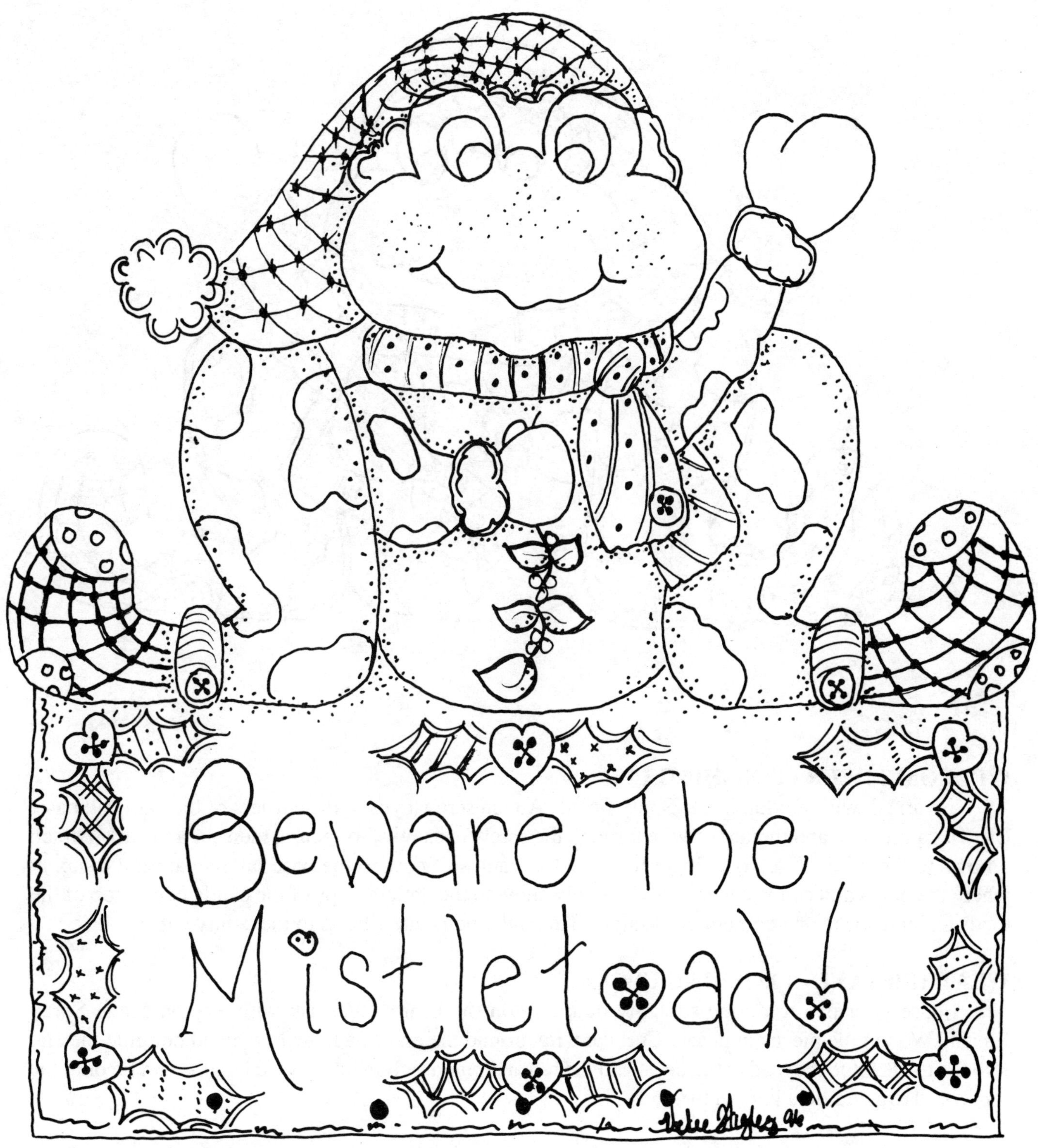

THE TOADS Continued

> **Sparkle Glaze**: Brush on the leaves.
> **Barn Red**: Float shade the socks, scarf and hat.
> **Tangerine**: Stipple the center of the knot on the scarf, the socks, and the top of the hat. Float highlight the top of the hat, and the top of the sock's cuffs.
> **Yellow**: Do the line work on the hat, scarf and socks.
> **White**: Dot the patches on the socks and the dots by the leaves.
> **14K Gold**: Dot the buttons on the scarf and socks and the tiny dots on the hat, scarf and socks. Line the ribbing on the sock cuffs.

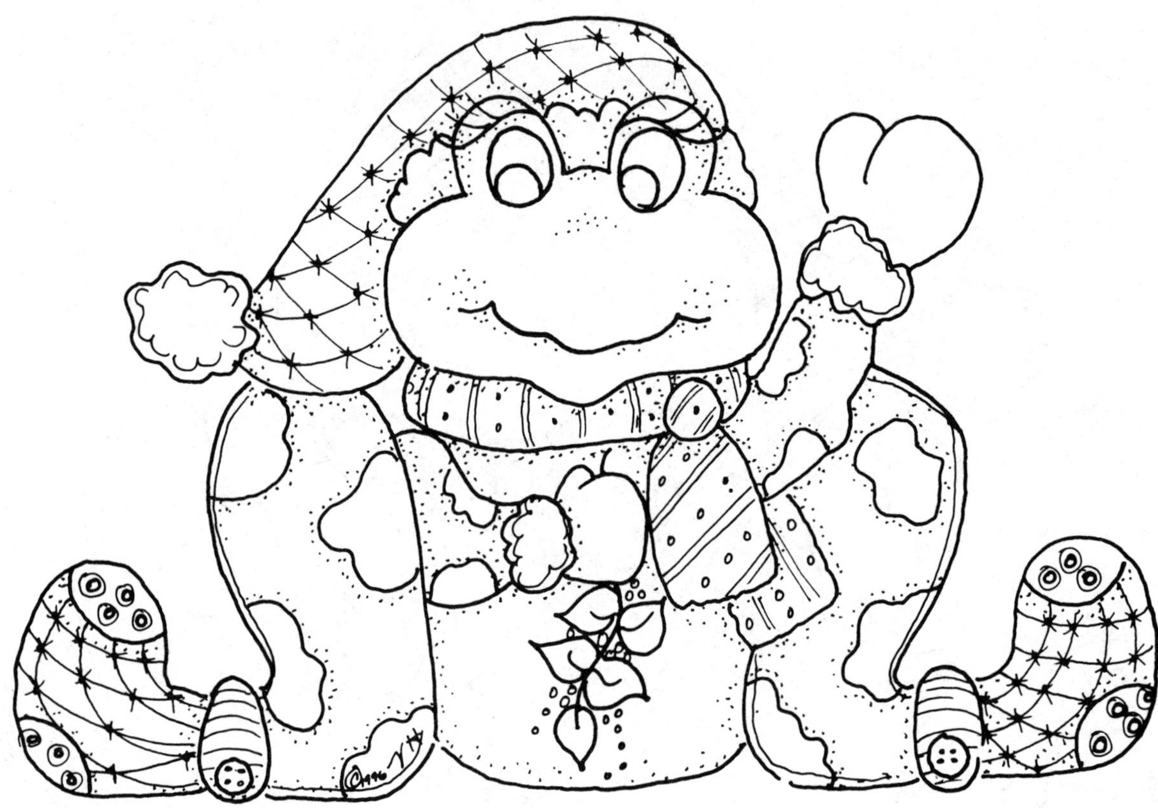

WELCOME DEER - FINISHING UP:

Varnish with Krylon Matte Spray finish. Attach screw eyes to the corners of the sign and base. Use 19 gauge wire and thread the wire through the screw eyes twist to secure, then cut and curl. Attach 2 bows to the wires. Use your finger to apply the Fantasy Snow to the base taking care not to apply where the boots and candy canes will sit. Apply snow to the antlers, tops of the candy canes, top of the toads hat and socks and corners of the sign. Tie on the bells and ribbon to the candy canes.

WEATHER VANE - FINISHING UP:

Use your pen to do the squiggly outlining on the hearts. Varnish with Krylon Matte Spray Finish. Wood glue pieces in place. Curl the wire around the end of a large brush and hot glue the end into the toad. Glue the toad to the deer. Cut the red and green ribbon into 1 yard lengths and tie onto the dowels. Trim and tie a knot in the ends.

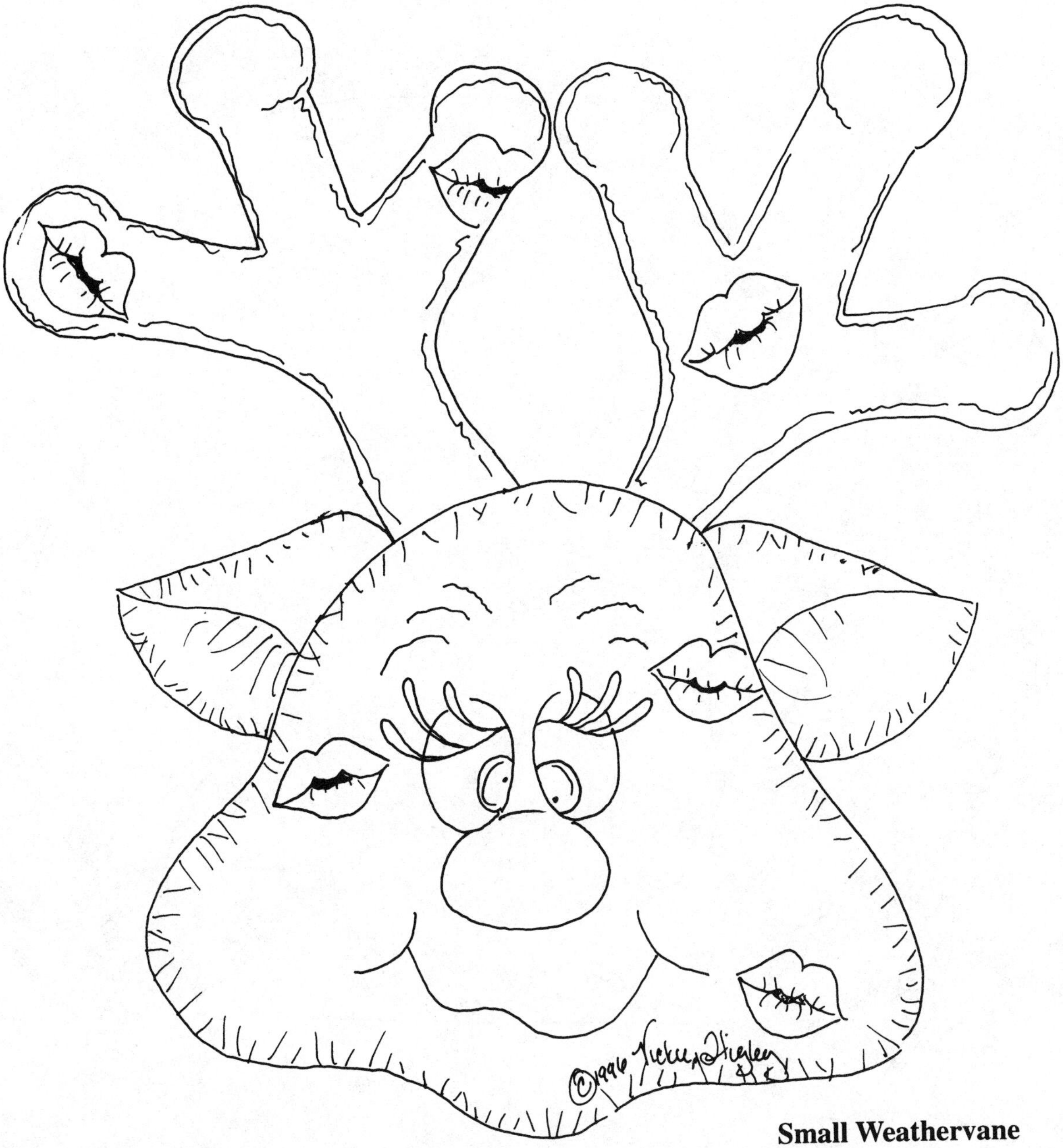

**Small Weathervane
Deer's Head - 1/2"**

WIND CHIME - FINISHING UP:

I sprayed the pipes with Krylon Black Spray Paint. Varnish the wood pieces with Krylon Matte Spray Finish. Attach the screw eyes to his hand and hat tassel. Cut and curl 2' of wire around the end of a large brush and thread through the screw eyes. Bend the ends around and cut off any extra wire.

PIPES

Cut and assemble according to the general directions.

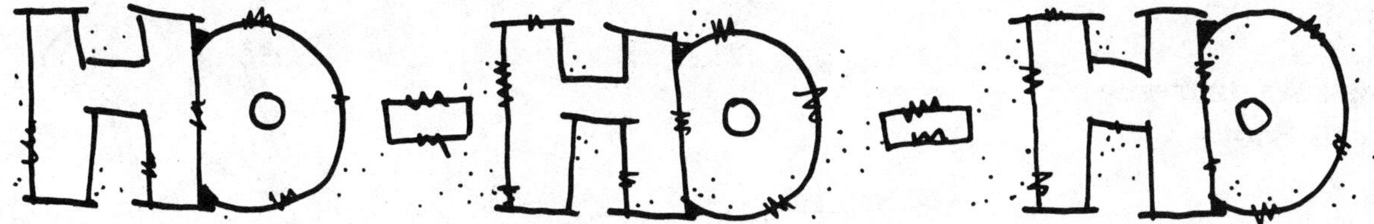

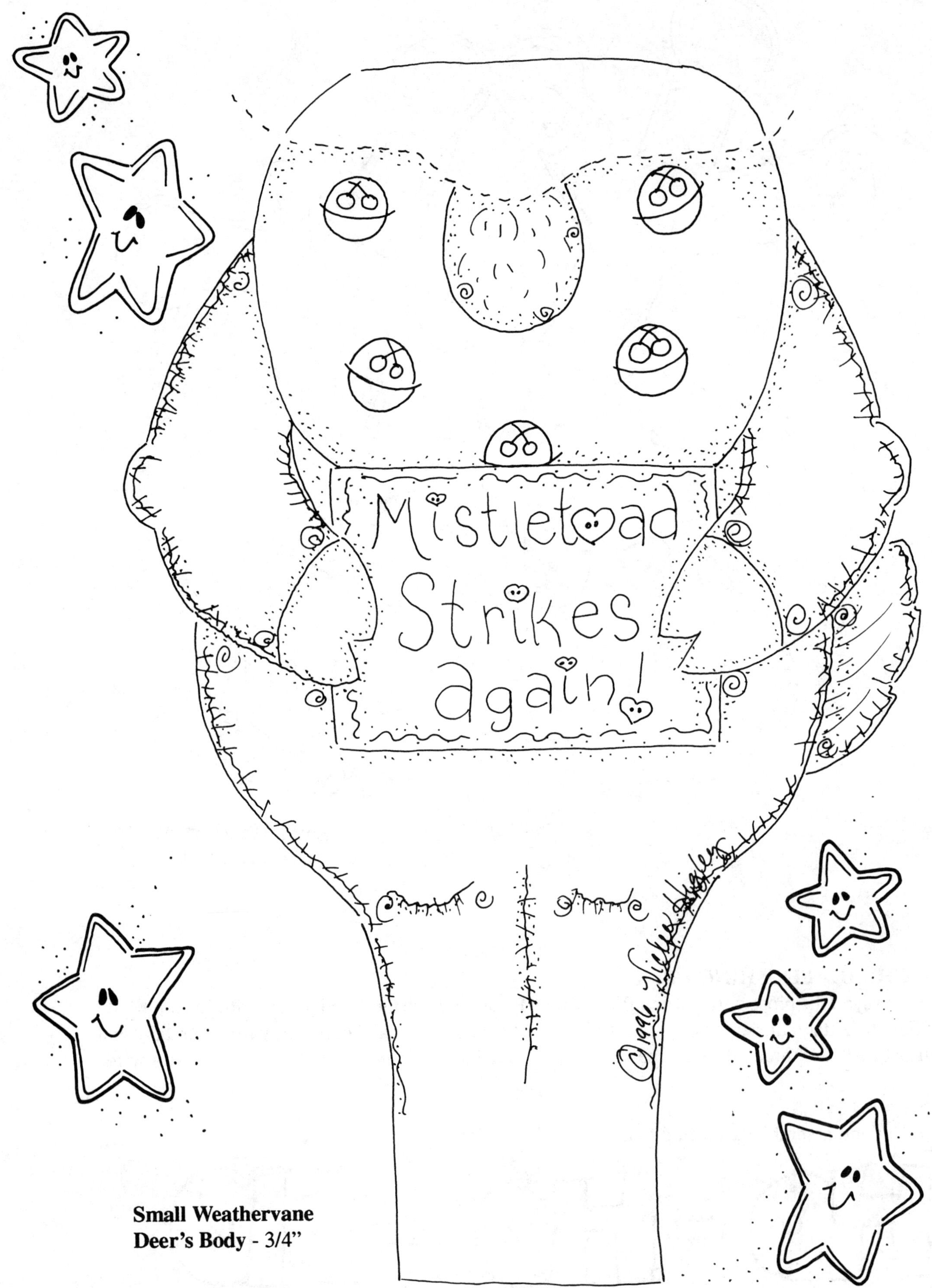

**Small Weathervane
Deer's Body - 3/4"**

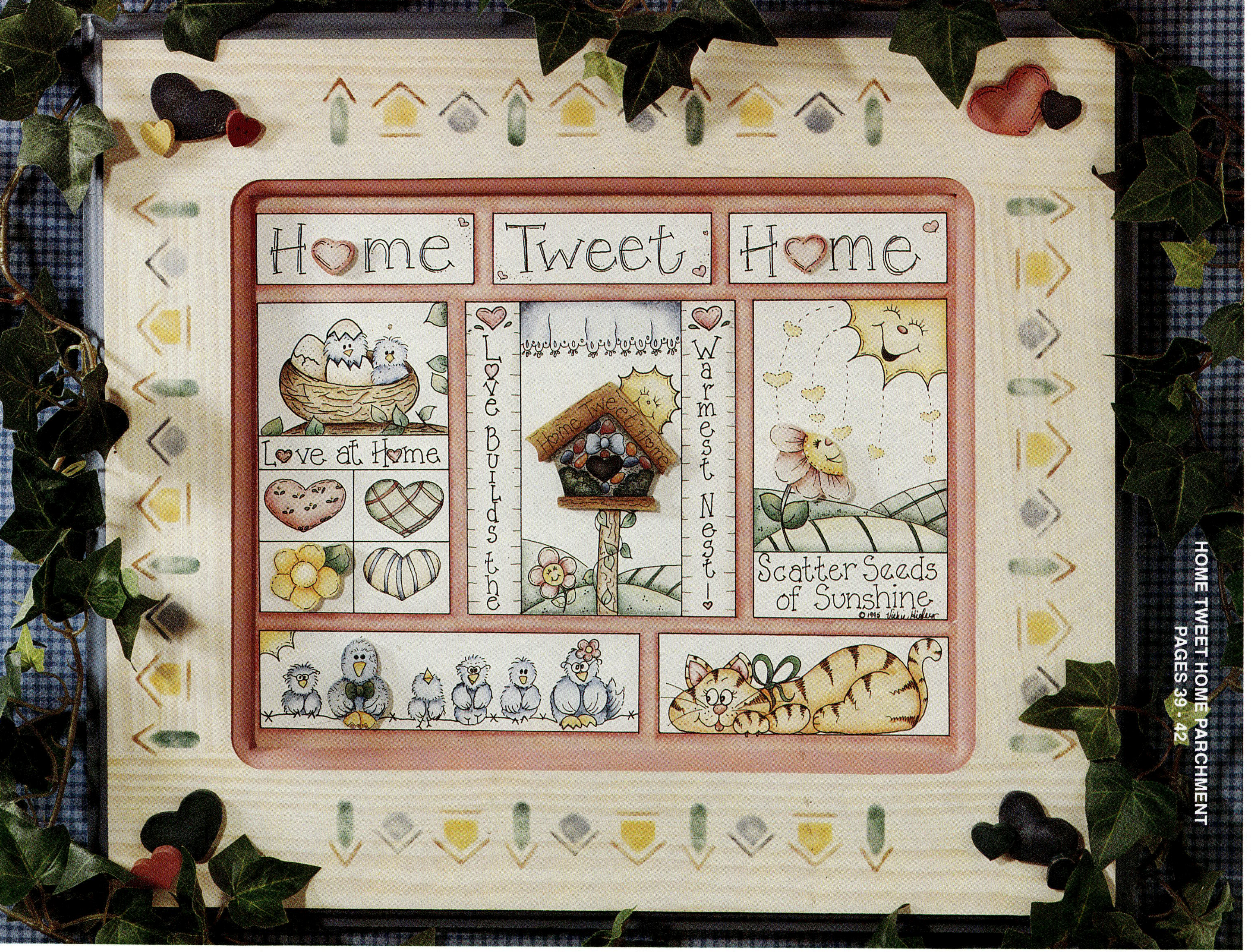
Home Tweet Home
Love at Home
Love Builds the
Home Tweet Home
Warmest Nest!
Scatter Seeds of Sunshine

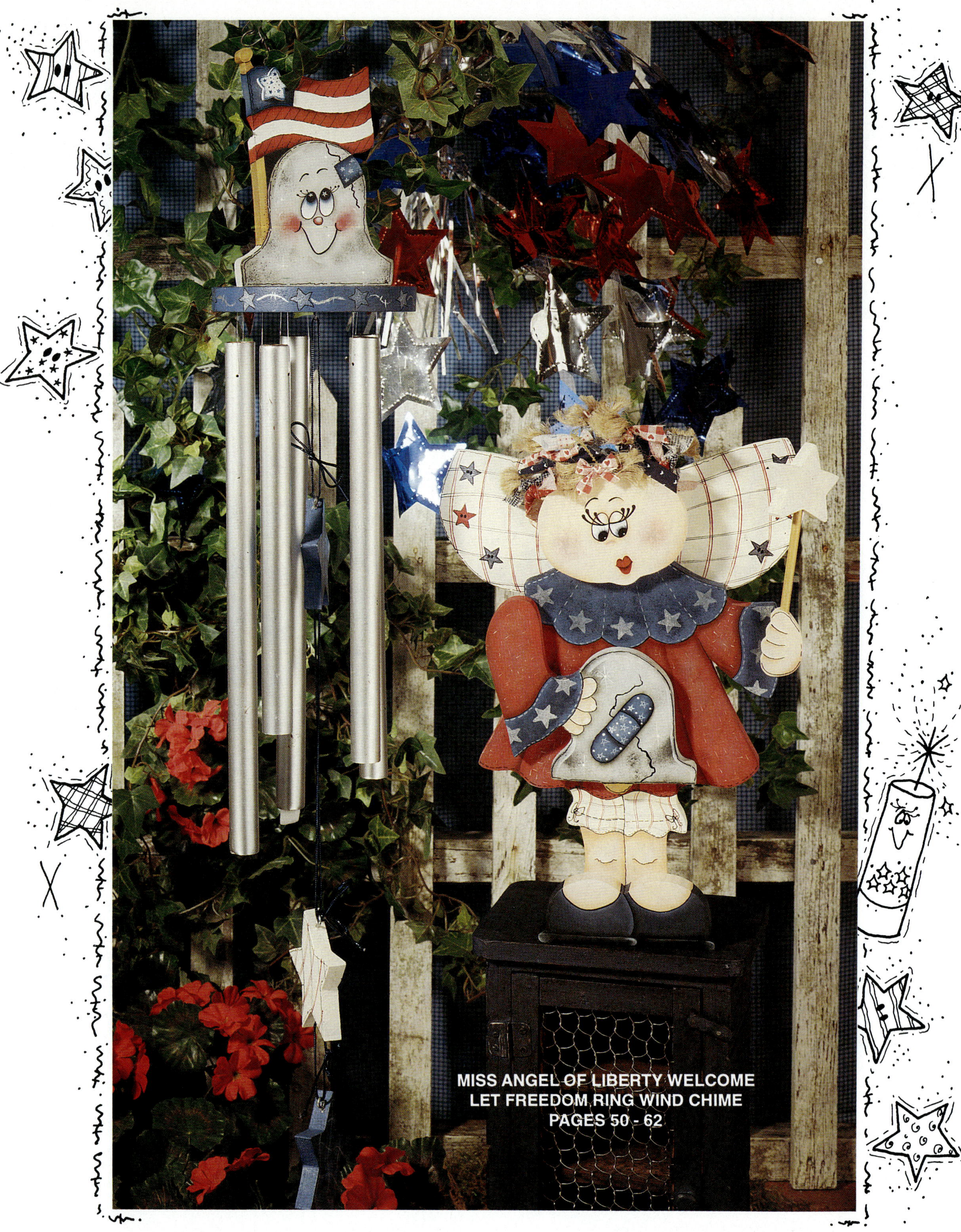

MISS ANGEL OF LIBERTY WELCOME
LET FREEDOM RING WIND CHIME
PAGES 50 - 62

HOME TWEET HOME PARCHMENT

PALETTE (DELTA)

Wild Rose	Barn Red	Spice Brown	Burnt Umber
Black	Crocus	Putty	White
Alpine	Cactus	Green Isle	Black Green
Hunter Green	Blue Danube	Denim Blue	Midnight
Sachet	Rose Mist	Drizzle Grey	Bittersweet
Hippo Grey	Georgia Clay	Pale Yellow	Tidepool
Woodland Night			

Provo Craft Stencil "Catch of the Day" No. 41-4906

Prepare the paper by spraying with three light mists of Krylon Matte Spray. Tape the edges to a piece of cardboard for painting ease. When painting on paper the first layer of color is the highlight so keep the washes very light. Mix the washes by using a bubble palette. I use 1/4 teaspoon of water to two drops of paint. Stir well with an old brush. Always touch your loaded brush to your paper towel before going to your parchment. This eliminates bleeding. After the color is washed in, side load float to shade the same as on wood.

The wood items are based opaque. Attach wood items to the paper with Tacky Glue after all painting is completed and wood has been sprayed with Krylon Matte Spray.

BORDER AND SMALL HEARTS

Wash with **Wild Rose**. Float shade **Barn Red**.

NEST BLOCK

Nest and Branch - wash **Spice Brown**. Float shade **Burnt Umber**. Deepen with **Burnt Umber + Black**. Float highlight nest **Crocus**.

Eggs - wash **Putty**. Float shade **Spice Brown**. Float highlight **White**.

Leaves - wash randomly, **Alpine, Cactus, Green Isle**. Float shade **Black Green** and **Hunter Green**.

Birds - wash **Blue Danube**. Float shade **Denim**, deepen **Midnight**.

Beaks - wash **Crocus**.

HEART AND FLOWER BLOCK

Wash top left heart **Sachet**. Float shade **Rose Mist**. Deepen **Barn Red**. Leaves - **Alpine**, Dots-**Crocus**.

Wash top right heart **Cactus**. Float shade **Alpine**. Lines-**Sachet**, float shade **Barn Red**.

Bottom right heart wash **Putty**. Float shade **Spice Brown**. Lines-**Blue Danube**, float shade **Midnight**.

Wood Flower - base **Crocus + White** (1:1). Stipple highlight **White**. Float shade **Bittersweet**. Center-base mix + **White**, float shade **Spice Brown**. Stipple the center **White**. Leaf-base **Cactus**. Float shade **Hunter Green**. Deepen **Black Green**. Highlight glaze **Crocus**.

HOME TWEET HOME PARCHMENT Continued

BIRD BLOCK

The birds are washed **Blue Danube**. Create different values by layering more **Blue Danube** on and shading some more heavily than others. Float shade **Denim Blue** and deepen with **Midnight**. Wash beaks and feet **Crocus**. Float shade **Crocus + Bittersweet**. Flower-wash **Sachet**. Float shade **Rose Mist**. Wash center **Crocus**. Sun-wash **Crocus**. Float shade **Crocus + Bittersweet**.

Wood Bird - base **Blue Danube**. Stipple **White**. Float shade **Denim Blue** and deepen with **Midnight**. Base beak and feet **Crocus**. Float shade **Bittersweet**. Float highlight **White**. Dot eyes **Black**.
Bow Tie-base **Green Isle**. Float shade **Black Green**. Float highlight **Crocus**.

CENTER BLOCK

Drizzle Grey-float the sides of the shutters. One strokes are **Alpine**.
Curtains - wash **Blue Danube**. Float shade **Denim Blue** and deepen with **Midnight**.
Sun-wash **Crocus**. Shade **Crocus + Bittersweet**. Nose-wash **Sachet**. Float shade **Barn Red**.
Grass-wash   area **Hunter Green**,   area **Alpine**,   area **Cactus**. Float shade **Black Green**. Float highlight **Crocus**.
Flower-wash **Sachet**. Float shade **Rose Mist**. Wash center **Crocus**. Wash leaves **Cactus**.
Pole-wash **Spice Brown**. Float shade **Spice Brown**.
Leaves-wash **Alpine** and **Cactus**. Float shade **Black Green** and **Hunter Green**.

Wood Bird House-wash roof and base **Spice Brown**. Float shade **Spice Brown**. Float highlight **Crocus**.
House-base **Drizzle Grey**.   Float shade **Hippo Grey.**
Bushes-base **Hunter Green**. Float shade **Black Green**. Stipple highlight **Cactus**. Stipple a smaller area **Crocus**.
Bow-base **Blue Danube**. Float shade **Denim Blue**. Deepen with **Midnight**. Float highlight **White**.
Opening-base **Hippo Grey**. Float shade **Black**.
Rocks-base some **Denim Blue**. Float shade **Midnight**. Float highlight **Blue Danube**. Base some Bittersweet. Float shade **Georgia Clay**. Float highlight **White**. Base some **Rose Mist**. Float shade **Barn Red**. Float highlight **White**. Dots are **Black**.

SUNSHINE BLOCK

Sun-wash **Crocus**. Float shade **Crocus + Bittersweet**. Nose-wash **Sachet**.
Grass (follow directions under CENTER BLOCK).
Leaves-wash **Hunter Green**. Float shade **Black Green**. Float highlight **Crocus**.

Wood Flower-base **Sachet + White (1:1)**. Float shade **Rose Mist** then deepen **Barn Red**. Stipple highlight then float highlight **White**. Center-base **Crocus + White (1:3)**. Float shade **Crocus + Bittersweet**. Stipple highlight **White**. Wash nose **Sachet**.

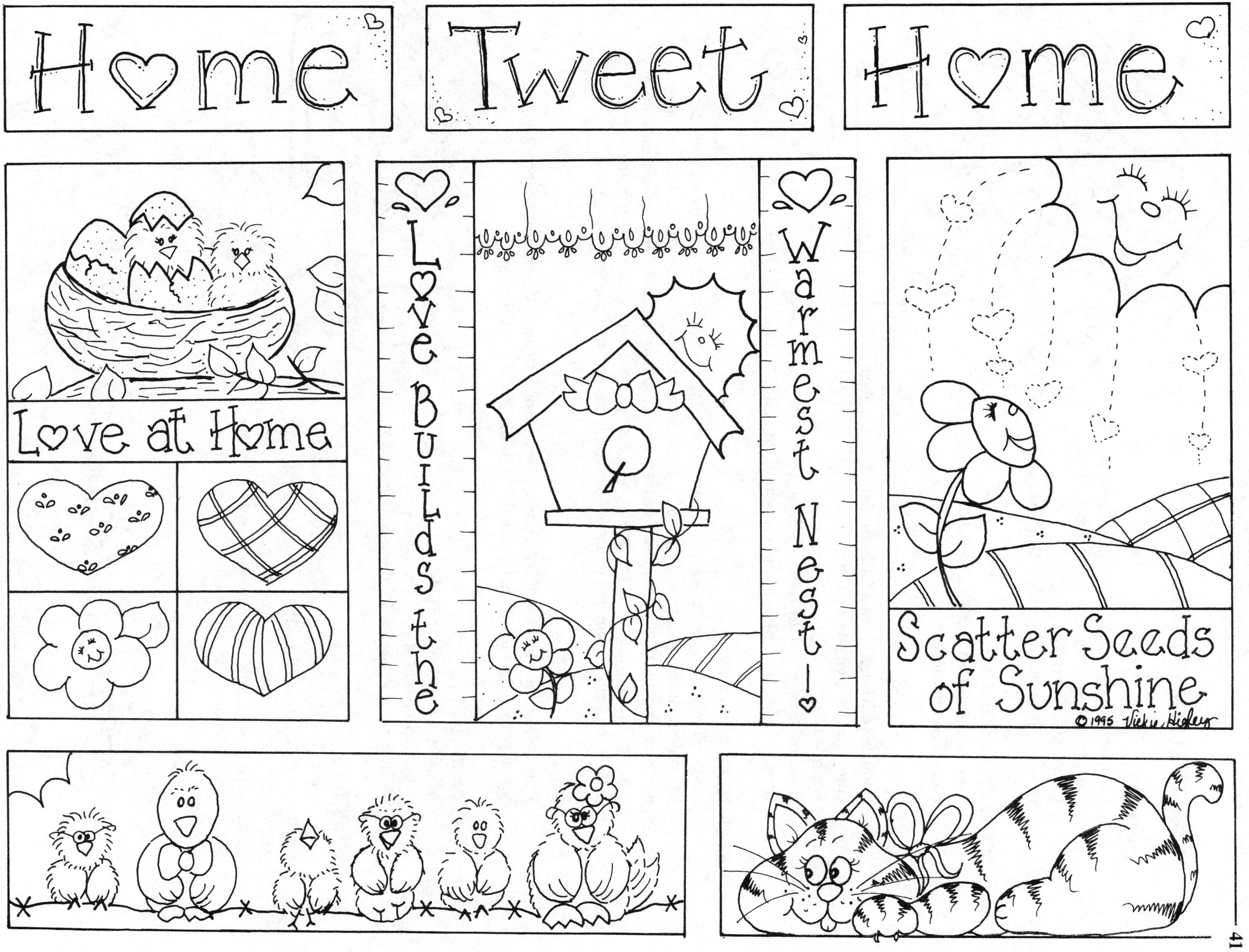

Home
Tweet
Home

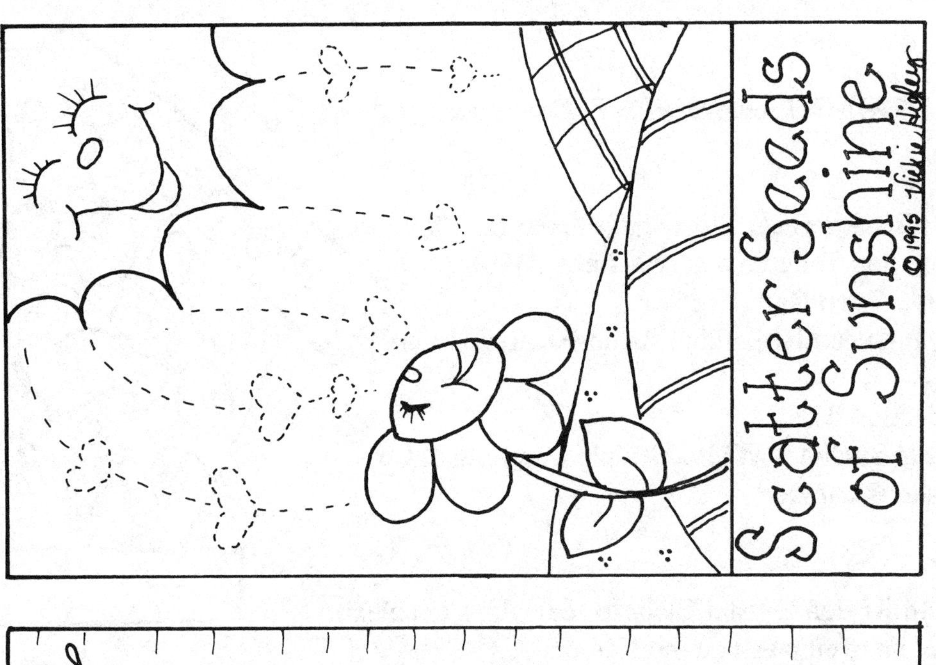

Scatter Seeds of Sunshine
©1995 Vicki Hicks
Warmest Nest
Love Builds the Spirit
Love at Home

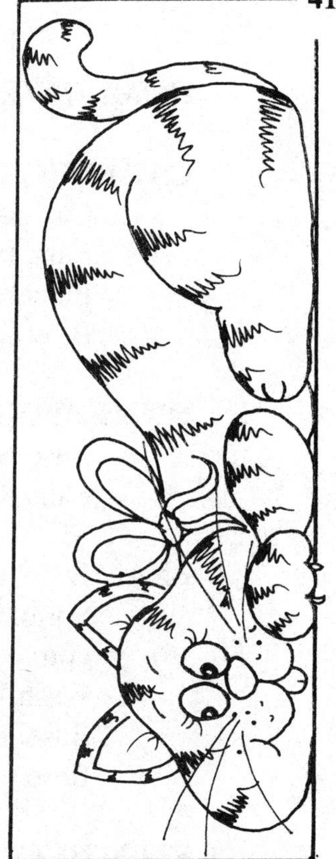

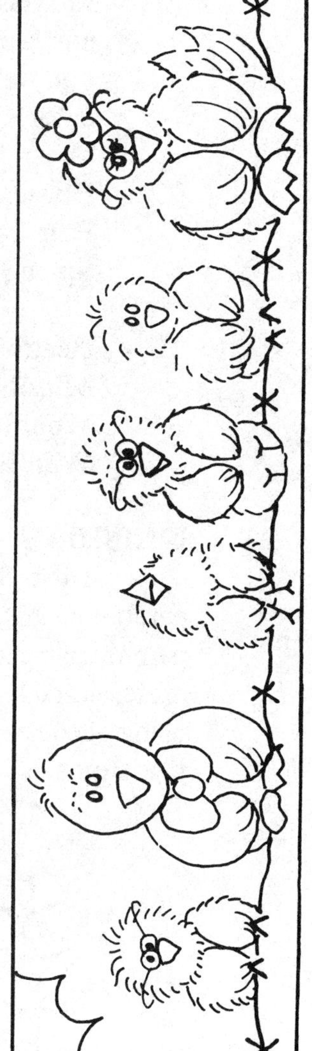

HOME TWEET HOME PARCHMENT Continued

CAT BLOCK

Cat-wash **Bittersweet**. Float shade **Georgia Clay**.
Ears, Nose and Tongue-wash **Sachet + White**.
Float shade **Barn Red**.
Bow-wash **Green Isle**. Float shade **Hunter Green**.

HOME WOOD HEARTS

Base hearts **Sachet + White**. Stipple highlight **White**.
Float shade **Barn Red**.

FRAME

Spray with Krylon Crystal Clear to seal. This enables
you to get an even wash on the frame.
Wash **White**
Base inside edge - **Wild Rose + White (1:1)**
Base outside edge - **Blue Danube + Midnight (1:1)**

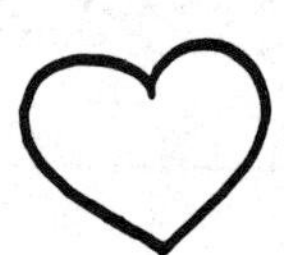

STENCIL DIRECTIONS

Mask off any areas on the stencil you won't be using with Scotch Magic Transparent tape.
Measure equal distance from both ends, position the stencil and tape down. Magic Transparent Tape won't lift the paint. Use a different stencil brush or fabric dye brush for each color
you will be using. You use the brush dry and don't want to clean the brush from color to
color. Use a circular motion to apply the paint to the surface. Use very little paint.

Houses
Pale Yellow then a touch of **Bittersweet**. Roof **Spice Brown, Woodland Night**. Roof
Spice Brown, **Tidepool**, then a touch of **Midnight**. Roof **Midnight**.

Hearts
Midnight-stipple **Blue Danube**.
Woodland Night-stipple **Cactus**.
Wild Rose + White - float **Barn Red** stipple **White**.

FINISHING

I use Scotch Spra-Ment (adhesive) to stick the
parchment to the board backing. This step keeps the
parchment nice and flat and gives the picture a finished
professional look. I fasten the board backing to the frame
using glazier's points. They are available at art and framing stores.

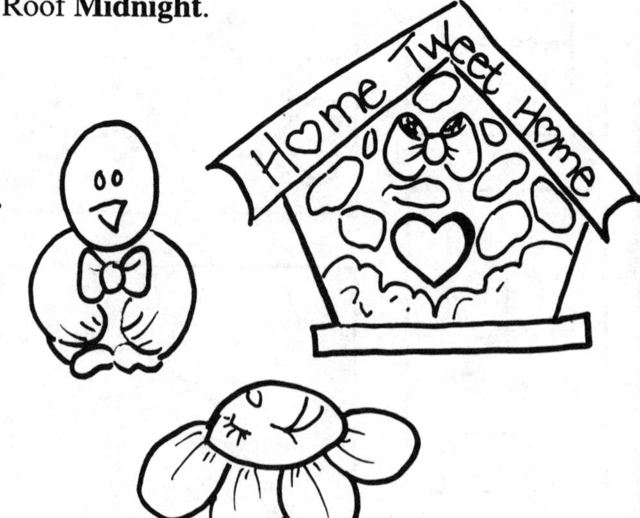

HE LOVES ME, HE LOVES ME NOT BIRDS

Follow the painting directions for the birds and nest from *Bird Chimes* project.

ADDITIONAL SUPPLIES

19 Gauge Wire   Green Floral Wire

LETTERING

Light Ivory: Base the letters. I used a No. 2 round.

Black: Use a liner and go over the letters letting the Light Ivory show through.

Burnt Umber: Use a liner and lightly put in the shadows behind the letters.

GARLAND LEAVES

Woodland Night: Wash the leaves. I used four of the No. 4, four of No. 3, one of No. 2, and one of No. 1.

FINISHING UP

Cut 18 inches of green floral wire and add the leaves one at a time, curling the wire as you go. Have some areas tighter than others. Attach the garland to the 19 gauge wire on the birds.

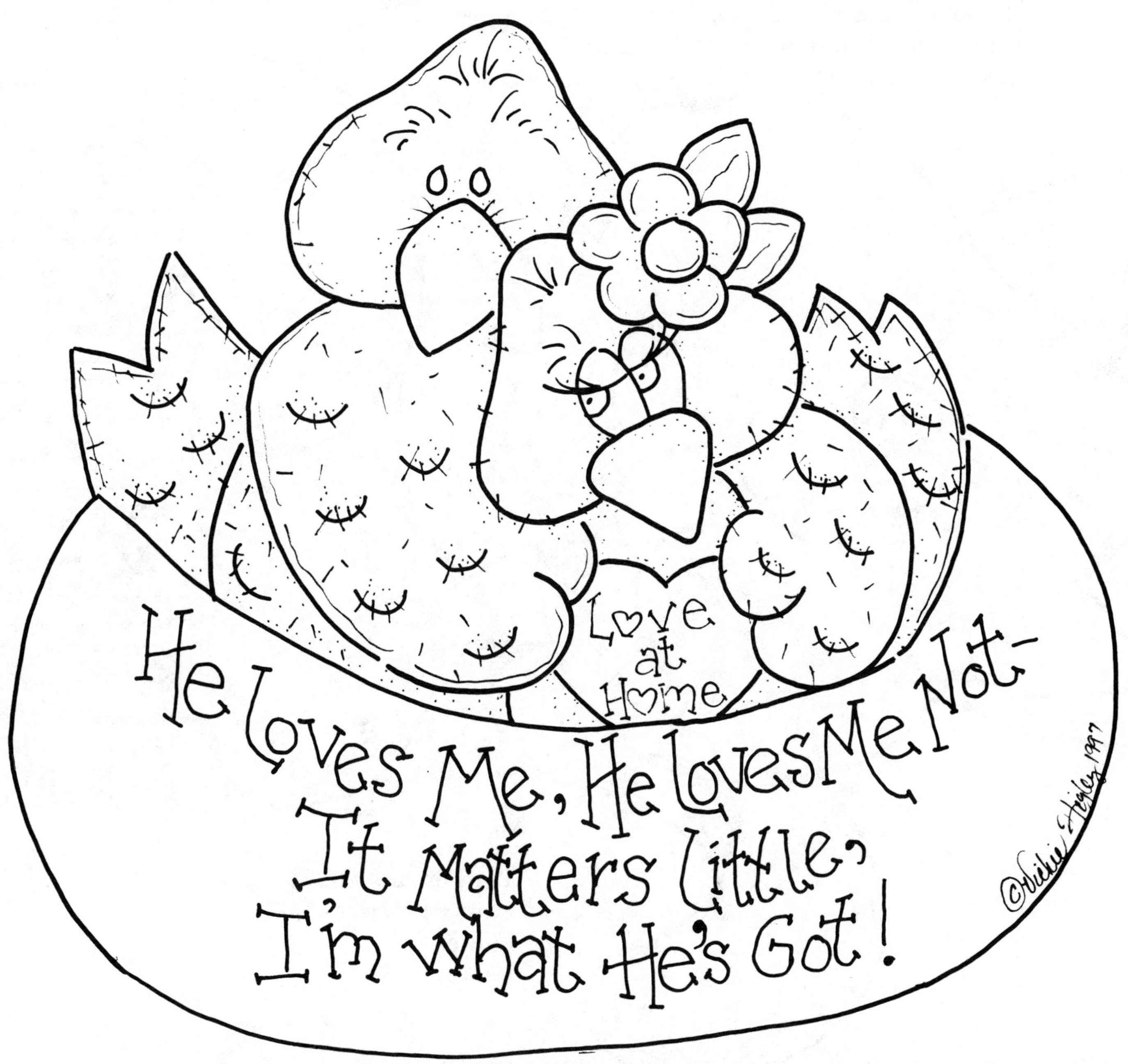

SWEET TWEETS COOKIE JAR LID
AND CLEAN YER PAWS PLEASE

PALETTE (DELTA)

Bittersweet	Georgia Clay	Crocus	Sachet
Black	14K Gold	Woodland Night	Barn Red
Blue Danube	Midnight	White	Hippo Grey
Burnt Umber	Light Ivory	Straw	

ADDITIONAL SUPPLIES FOR CLEAN YER PAWS PLEASE

2-1/2 Feet of 19 Gauge Wire   Green Floral Wire

Follow the painting directions for the cat in *Welcome Birdhouse* with these additions:

White: Base the feathers and stroke the fur. I used a No. 2 round for the feathers.

Hippo Grey: Flat shade the feathers and do the linework.

Straw: Underbase the name tag.

14K Gold: Base the name tag.

Burnt Umber + Barn Red:
Flat shade the name tag.

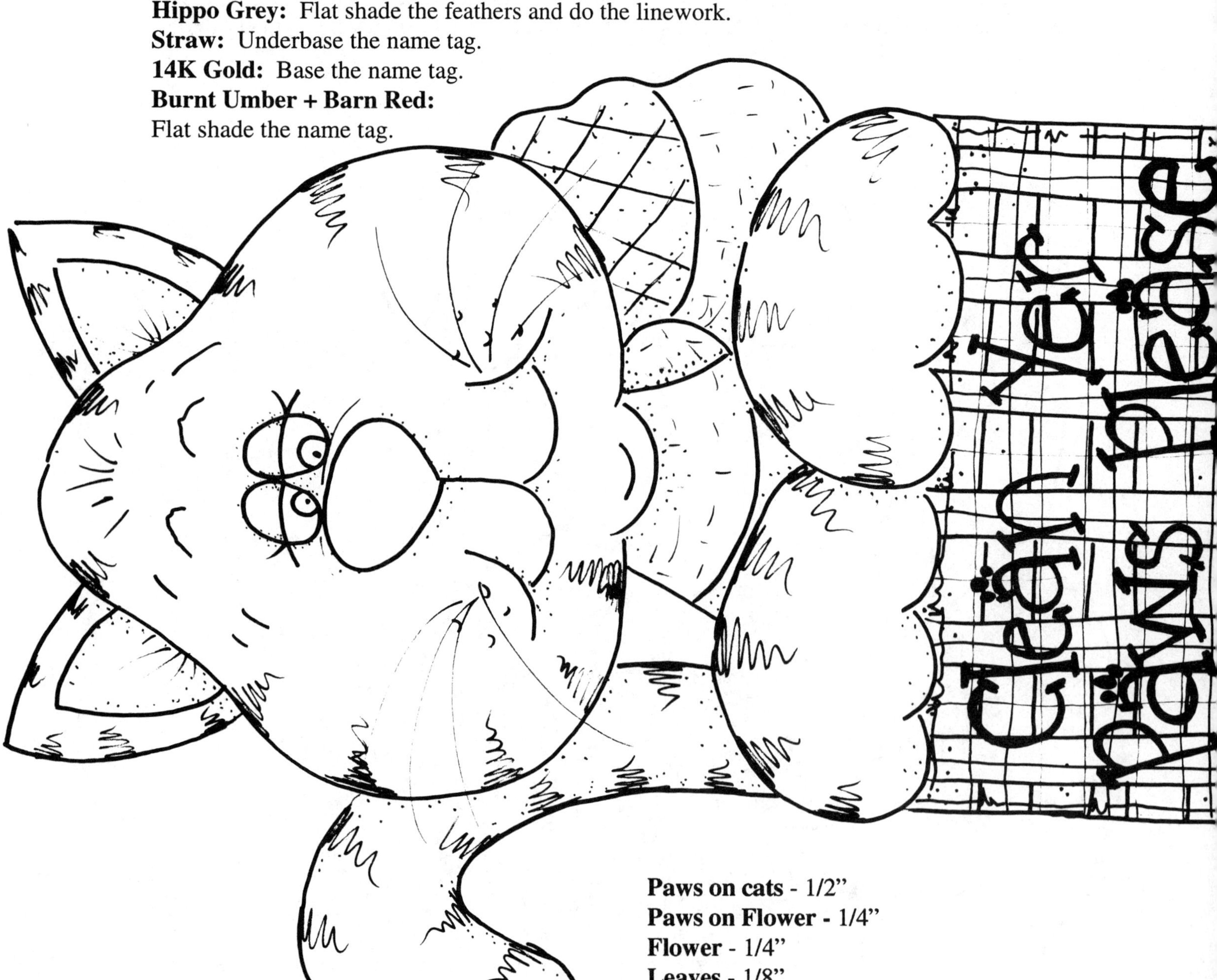

Paws on cats - 1/2"
Paws on Flower - 1/4"
Flower - 1/4"
Leaves - 1/8"

SWEET TWEETS COOKIE JAR LID AND CLEAN YER PAWS PLEASE Continued

FOOT PADS

Sachet + White: base the pads.
Barn Red: Stipple the center of the pads and float shade the bottom of the pads.
White: Float highlight the top of the pads.
The **CLEAN YER PAWS PLEASE** cat's paws are dry brushed with **Burnt Umber**.

SIGN

Light Ivory: Base the sign.
Plaid: Thin all the paint so it flows freely from the brush. Wait until each layer is dry before proceeding.
Blue Danube: Wash in the plaid using a No. 8 flat.
Midnight: Do the linework on the Blue danube areas.
Crocus: Do the remaining linework.
Black: Do the lettering with a No. 2 round.

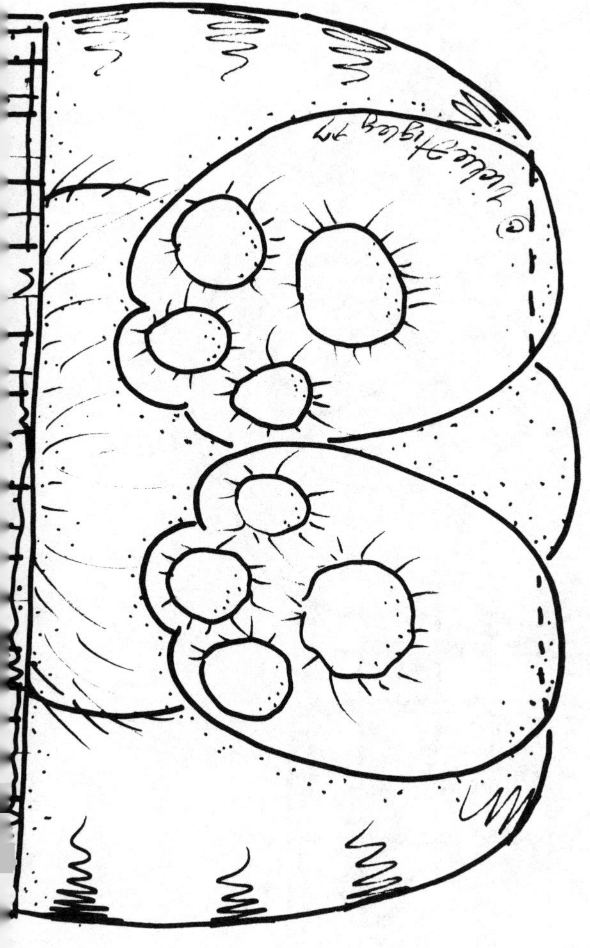

Cookie Lid Finishing Up

Use wood glue to attach the paws and the round to the back. I used a Pigma Micron 15 pen for the linework on the cat and the .08 for the sign. Spray with Kryon Matte Spray Finish.

CLEAN YER PAWS PLEASE FLOWER

Follow the painting directions for *Birdhouse Welcome*.
LEAVES: With **Woodland Night** wash the leaves.

CLEAN YER PAWS PLEASE FINISHING UP

Use wood glue to attach the paws. Curl 2-1/2 feet of 19 gauge wire around a large brush and attach to the cat. Cut seven inches of green floral wire to attach the paws to the flower. Use various sizes of the leaves to make the garland. I used three of No. 1 , two of No. 2, three of No. 3 and one of No. 4. Spray with Krylon Matte Spray Finish.

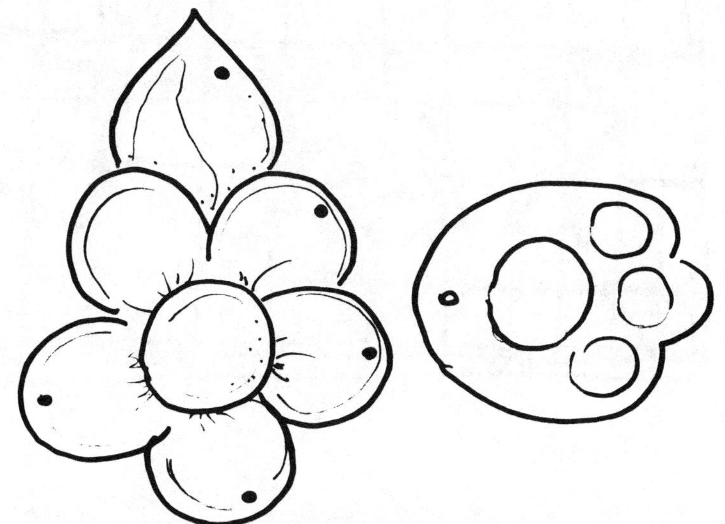

46

Cookie Lid requires 3 1/2" circle.
Paws are seperate - 1/2"

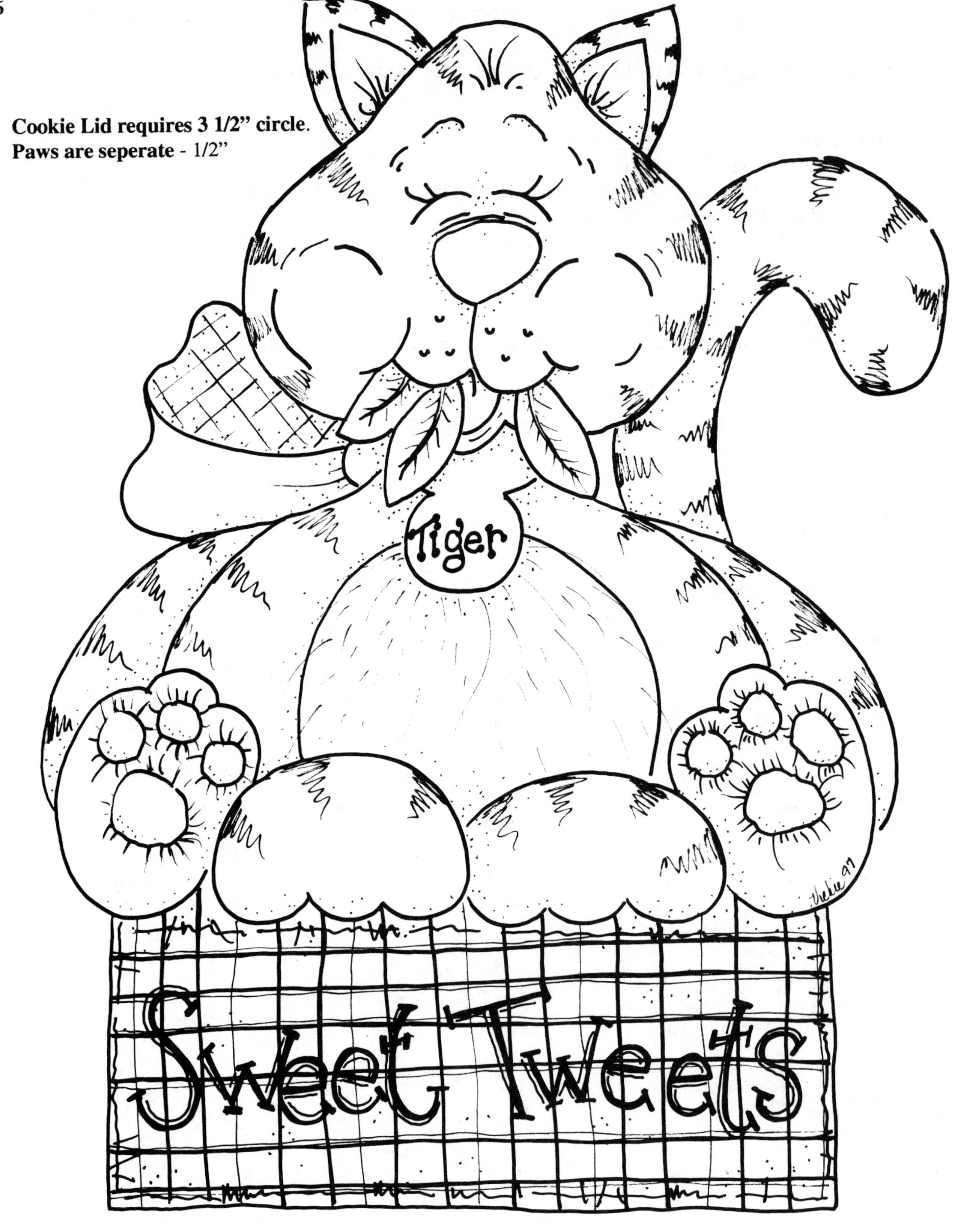

FLOWER POT BIRD HOUSES

PALETTE (Delta)

Spice Brown	Hunter Green	Blue Danube	White
Barn Red	Burnt Umber	Crocus	Lime Green
Denim blue	Bittersweet	Sachet	Hippo Grey
Drizzle Grey	Cactus	Midnight	Georgia Clay
Wild Rose	Nightfall	Black Green	Black
Rose Mist	Tomato Spice	Woodland Night	

ADDITIONAL SUPPLIES

Green Floral Wire	19 Gauge Wire 7" long	5" Clay Pot
Spanish Moss	Plant	Styrofoam

1/4" Dowel cut into the following lengths: 3-1/2", 4,", 6-1/2", 9"
1/8" Dowel cut into the following lengths: 2", three 5-1/2"
Provo Craft Stencil "Catch of the Day" No. 41-4906
Five Wood Pots Available From Plum Fun Wood Products No. FP202
1/4" Drill bit for hole in the bottom of each pot.

ROCK BIRD HOUSE

Paint according the directions for *Birdhouse Welcome*.

BOW

Blue Danube: Base the bow.
Midnight: Float shade.
White: Float highlight.

SUN, CAT and FLOWERS

Paint according to the directions for *Birdhouse Welcome*.

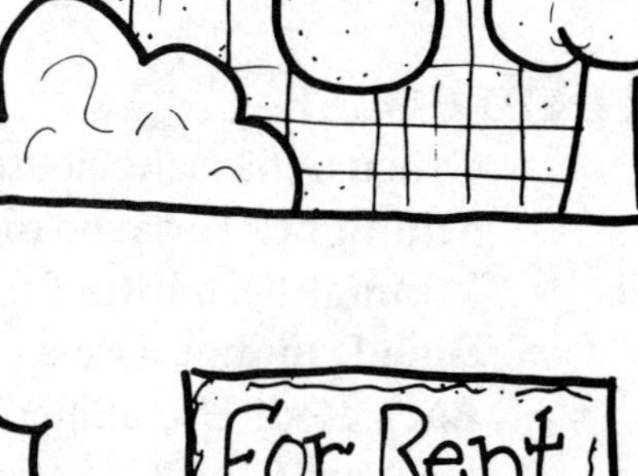

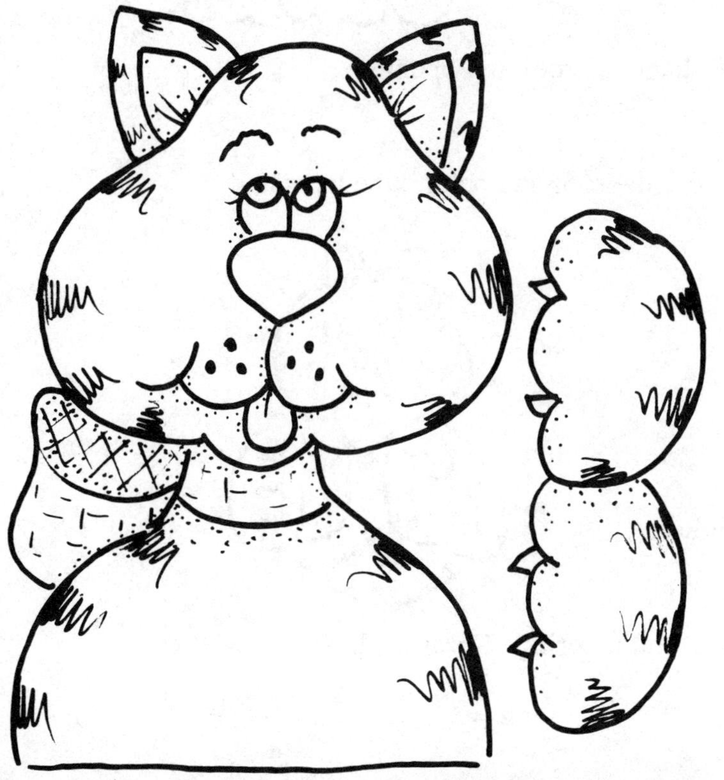

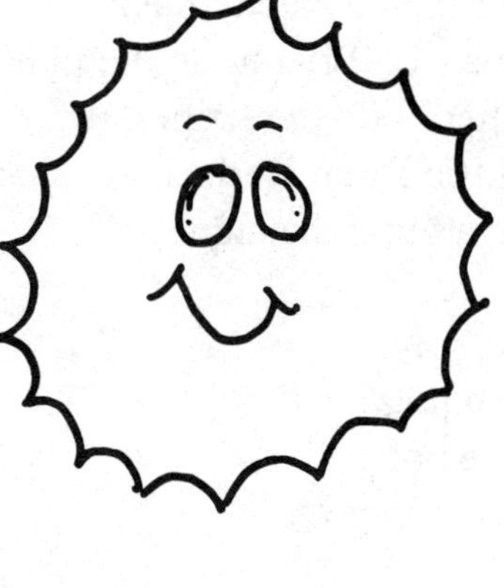

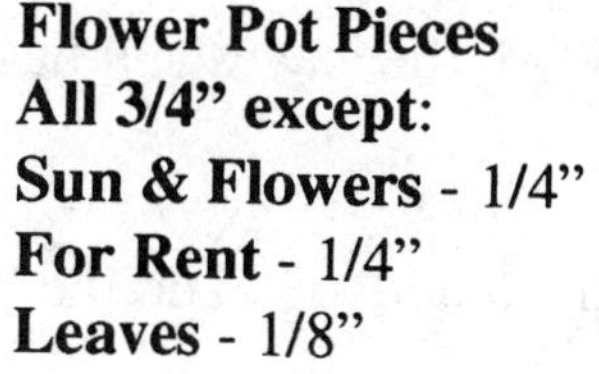

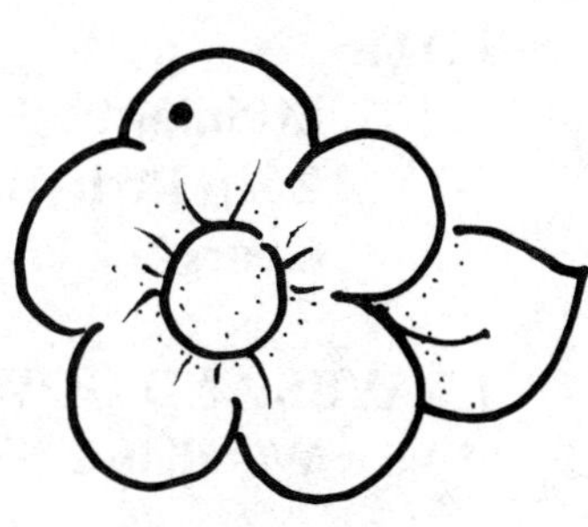

Flower Pot Pieces
All 3/4" except:
Sun & Flowers - 1/4"
For Rent - 1/4"
Leaves - 1/8"

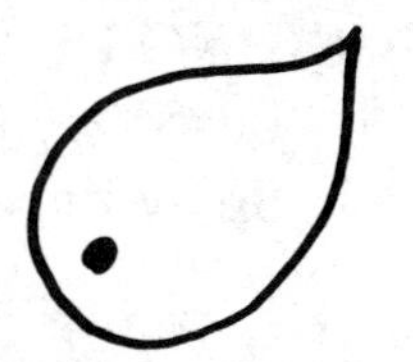

FLOWER POT BIRD HOUSES Continued

POT

Light Ivory: Base the pot.
Stencil the top of the pot. The green houses are **Woodland Night**, the yellow houses are **Crocus**; both with **Burnt Umber** roofs. The blue houses are **Midnight** with **Midnight** roofs.
Do the plaid according to the directions in Sweet Tweets Cookie Jar Lid.
Burnt Umber: Fly speck the pot.
I used a Pigma Micron .09 to do the linework.
Spray with Krylon Matte Spray Finish.

SCHOOL

Tomato Spice: Wash the school.
Spice Brown: Wash the roof.
Drizzle Grey: Base the shingles and the openings.
Burnt Umber: Float shade the roof.
Hippo Grey: Float shade the shingles and the openings. Then add a little **Black** and deepen.
Barn Red: Float shade the school.
Drizzle Grey: Thin the paint and use a liner to give the faint appearance of bricks.

BUSHES AND TREE

Hunter Green + Lime Green: Base the bushes.
Black Green: Stipple the bottoms and then float shade.
Lime Green: Float highlight here and there.
Crocus: Lightly stipple in the highlight areas.
Burnt Umber: Base the tree trunk and the "For Rent" stick.

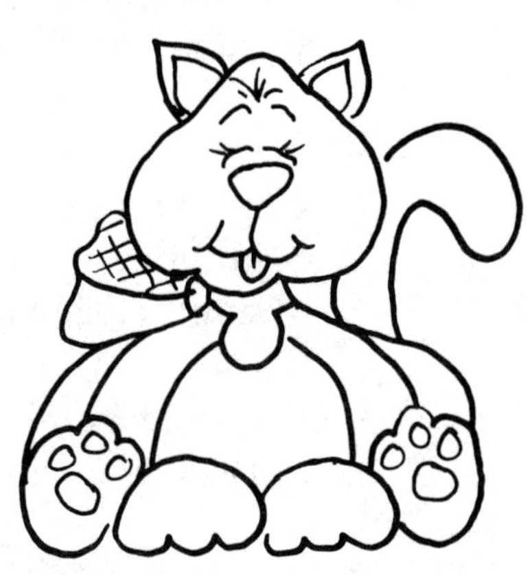

PLAID HOUSE

Crocus: base the house and the sign.
Midnight: Base the roof and the openings.
Midnight + a little Black: Palette blend and float shade the roof and openings.
Blue Danube: Use a No. 2 flat to do the plaid.
Barn Red: Use a liner to do the stripes.
Georgia Clay + a little Barn Red: Float shade under the roof and behind the trees and bushes.Lightly float around the sign.

POTS

Midnight: Base two pots.
Barn Red: Base one pot.
Georgia Clay: Base two pots.

LEAVES AND DOWELS

Woodland Night: Wash the leaves and base the dowels.

FINISHING UP

I used Pigma Micron .05 and .08 to do the line work and lettering. Spray with Krylon Matte Spray finish.

FLOWER POT BIRD HOUSES Continued

ROCK HOUSE ASSEMBLY DIRECTIONS

Curl the 19 gauge wire and glue to the sun to the roof.
Glue the nine inch dowel into the house.
Twist about 7 inches of green wire under the house. Wire on the leaves.
Slide on the Georgia Clay Pot, two more leaves, then the Midnight Pot. Fill the pots with the moss.
Curl green wire down the dowel.

School and Plaid House Assembly Directions:
Use the three 1/2" dowels between the houses and assemble as for the Rock House.
Cat
Curl two leaves onto wire and attach to the top of his head. (He thinks he's camoflaged!)
Glue the 1/4" dowl into him and hot glue the paws to the front of the pot.
Flowers
Start at the top of the 1/8" dowels and wind the green onto the dowel. Attach the flower at the top and add the leaves as you go down. You can add separate little curls of wire if you desire.

Arrange all with a plant in the pot!

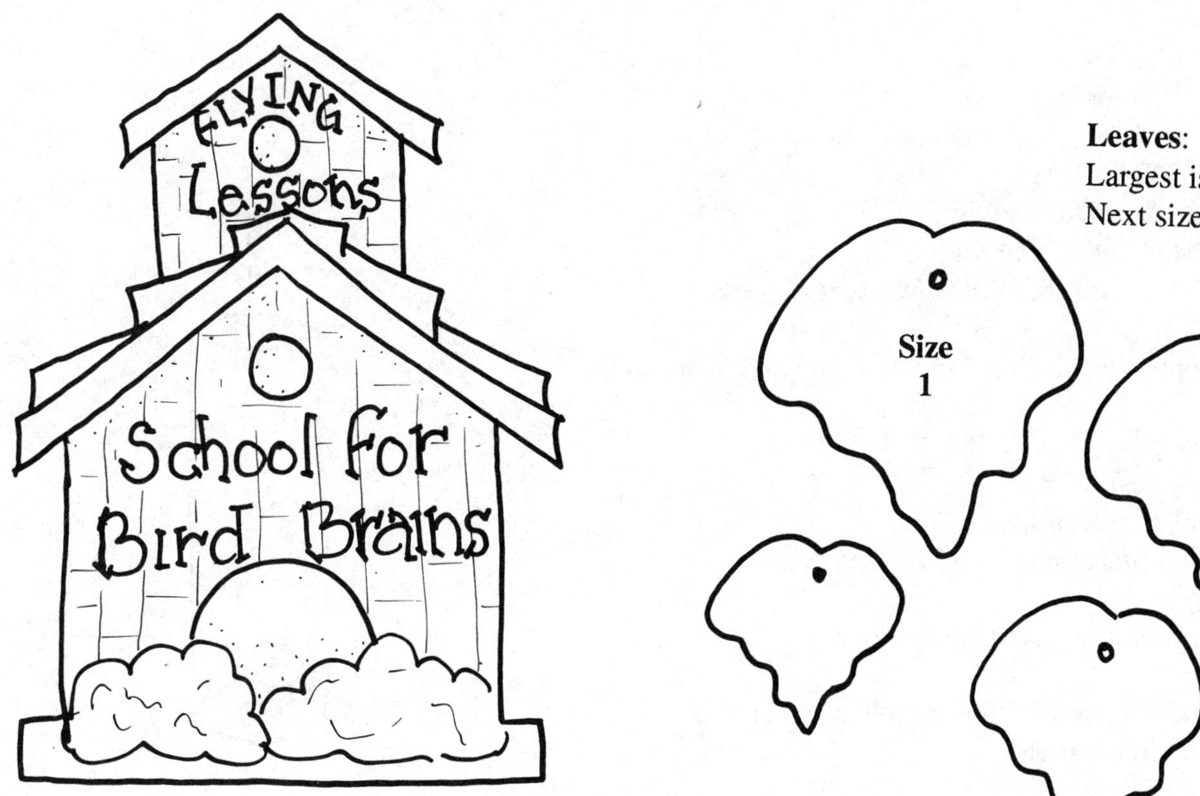

Leaves:
Largest is #1
Next size down is #2, etc.

Size
1

Painting directions for:

Miss Angel of Liberty Welcome
Let Freedom Ring Wind Chime
Liberty Bell Weather Vane

PALETTE (by Delta)

Santa's Flesh   Medium Flesh   Gleams Silver   Barn Red
Black   Gleams 14 K Gold   White   Bittersweet
Denim Blue   Midnight   Lt. Ivory   Old Parchment
Drizzle Grey   Hippo Grey   Charcoal   Straw
Spice Brown

Additional Supplies Needed for Miss Liberty Welcome:

6 Pieces of Jute for Hair each 2 1/2" long
11, 1/2" Strips of Coordinating Fabric
Hair Bows each 5" long
12" of 1/4" Dowel for flag pole
5" and 4" of 1/4" dowel for stars
1/2" wood ball for flag pole
24" of Blue and Silver Metallic Cording for bows on the sign
2' of 19 gauge wire
4 screw eyes
Wood glue

Plum Fun Stars: Item #

O SA326 6 for Wings (opt)
Q SA329 4 for Large Stars on dowels
K ST415 3 for Flags
F ST407 2 for Justice Sign
C ST404 1 for Justice Sign
A ST400 2 for Liberty Bell Weather Vane

Additional Supplies needed for Let Freedom Ring Wind Chime:

Pipes
8 screw eyes
2' of 19 gauge wire
2 yds. of Blue Cording
Plum Fun Star Item # K ST415 for flag
Fishing line
Krylon Metallic Silver Spray Paint

Additional Supplies needed Liberty Bell Weather Vane:

Metallic Star Garland
Blue and Silver Metallic Cording cut 6 pieces of each color 33" long
Wood glue

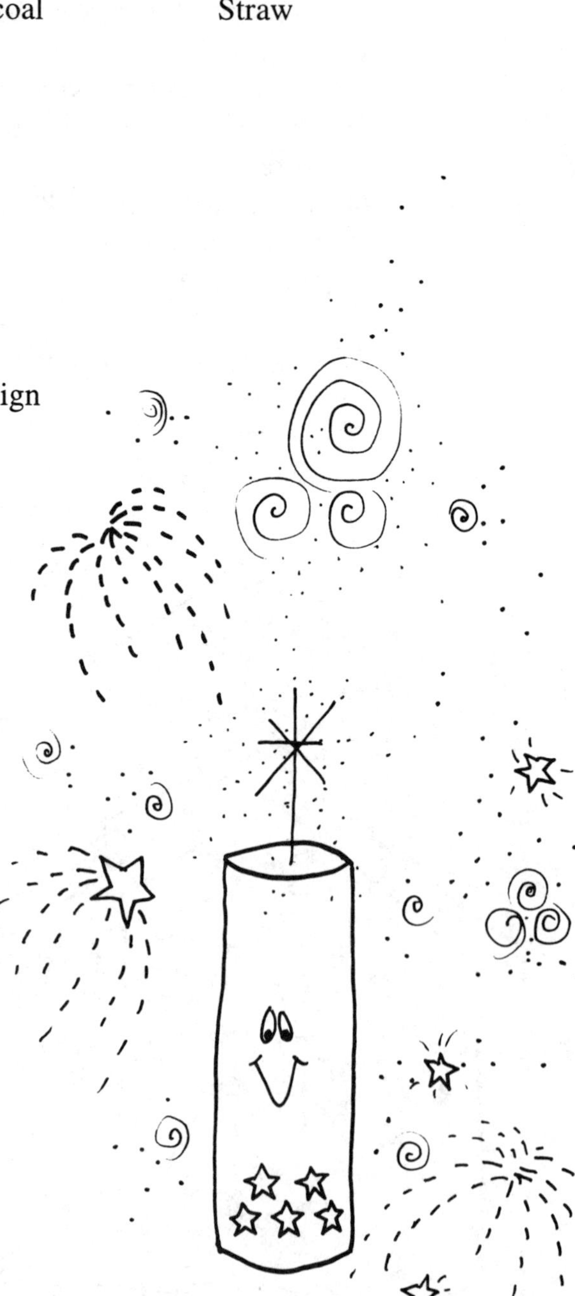

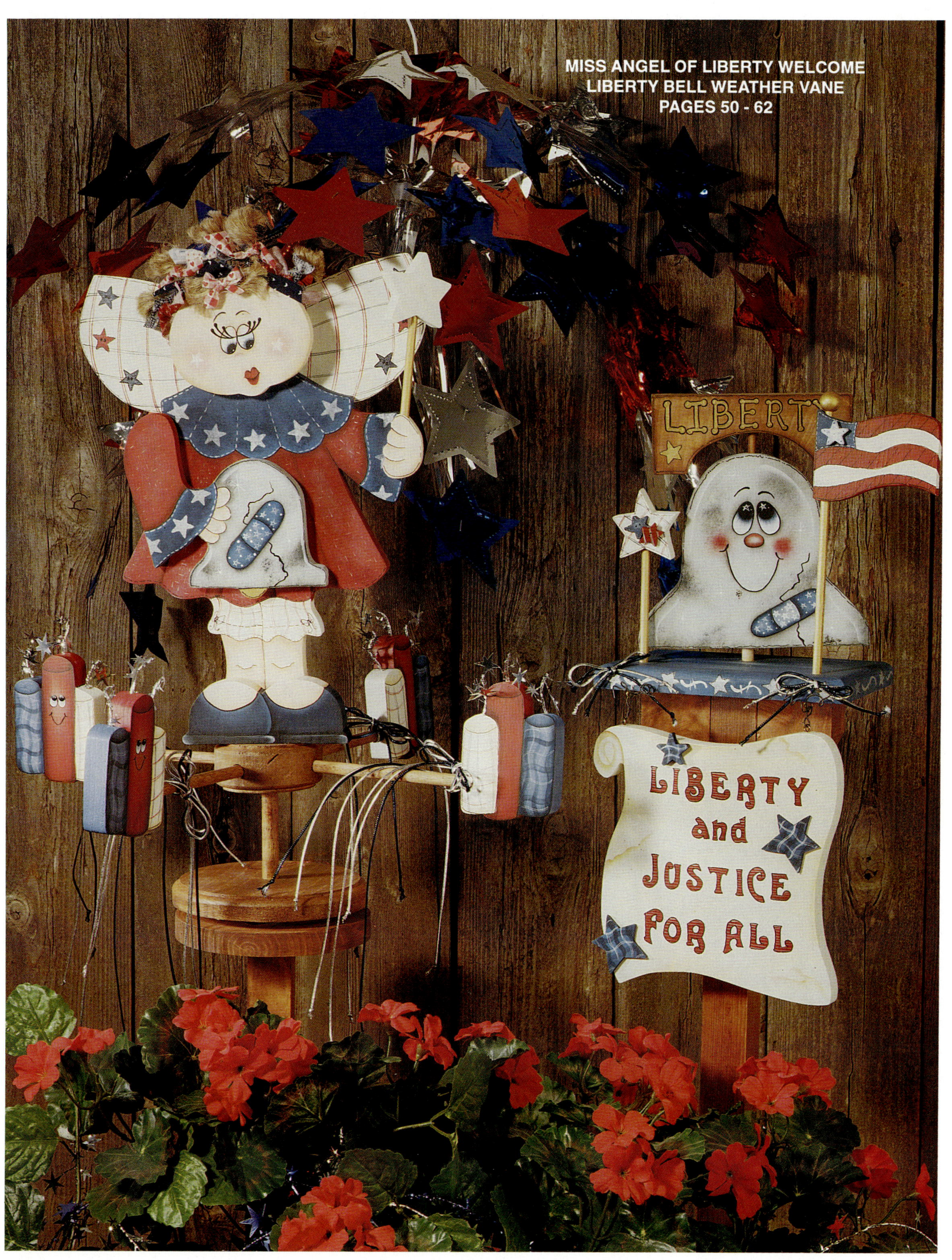
MISS ANGEL OF LIBERTY WELCOME
LIBERTY BELL WEATHER VANE
PAGES 50 - 62
LIBERTY
LIBERTY
and
JUSTICE
FOR ALL

Miss Liberty's Welcome Sign - 3/4"
Large Star Welcome - 1/8"
Small Star Welcome - 1/4"

ALL BELLS

Spice Brown: Wash the wood area of the Weather Vane Bell.
Drizzle Grey: Base the bell.
Hippo Grey: Stipple the shadows on the bell.
Charcoal + a little **White**: Stipple again, this time in a smaller area.
Hippo Grey: Float shade all around the bell, around the band-aid, eyes, and under the nose and mouth.
Charcoal: Deepen the float under the bottom of the band-aid.
White: Base the eyes.
Black: Base the pupils.
Denim Blue: Float shade the iris.
Midnight: Float shade to deepen the shade in the iris then do the lines in the iris.
Barn Red: Base the nose and stipple the cheeks.
Candy Bar: Float shade the bottom of the nose.
White: Stipple the center of the nose.
Denim Blue: Base the band-aid.
Midnight: Float shade all the way around the band-aid and behind the sides of the center section.
White: Stipple the band-aid, stipple the center area more heavily.
Float the highlights on the bell, do the twinkle stars on the bell, the stars and dots in the eyes and on the band-aid.
Straw: Undercoat the ringer and the letters on the Welcome bell.
14 K Gold: Base the ringer and the letters.
Black: Line the mouth, nose, eyes and eyebrows, crack, and band-aid.
Use a pen to do the squiggly outlining.

Liberty Chimes - 3/4"

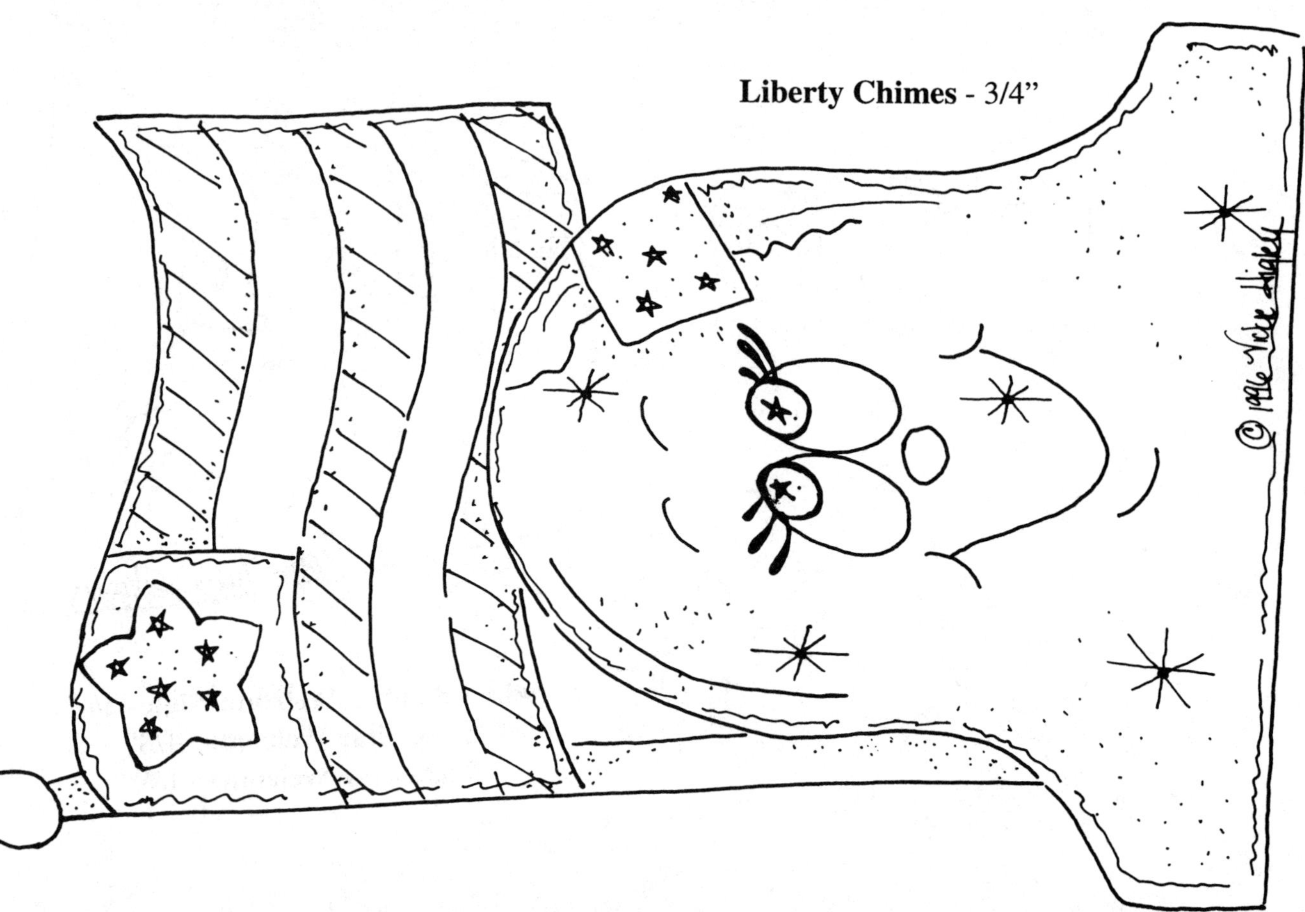

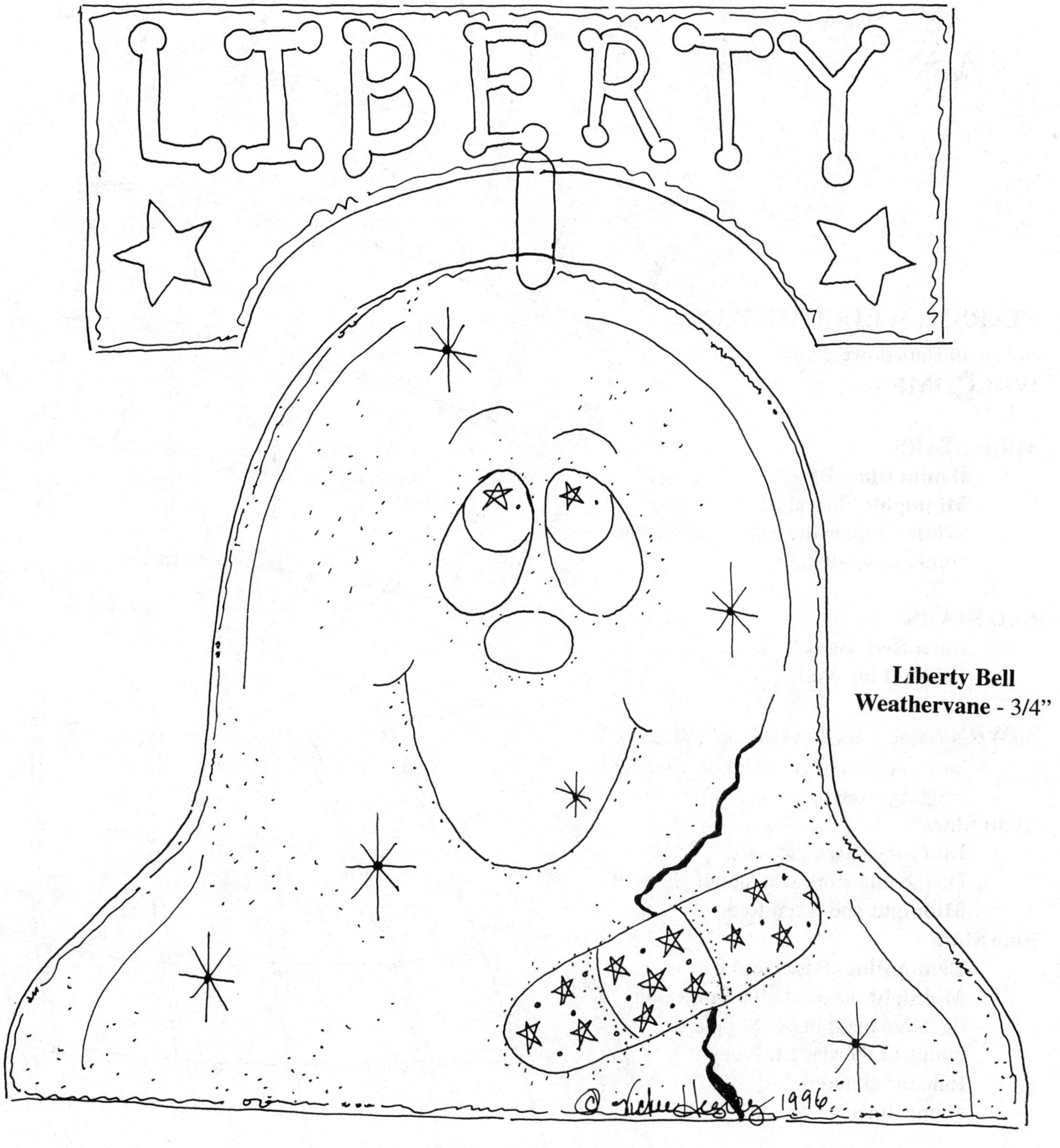

Let Freedom Ring

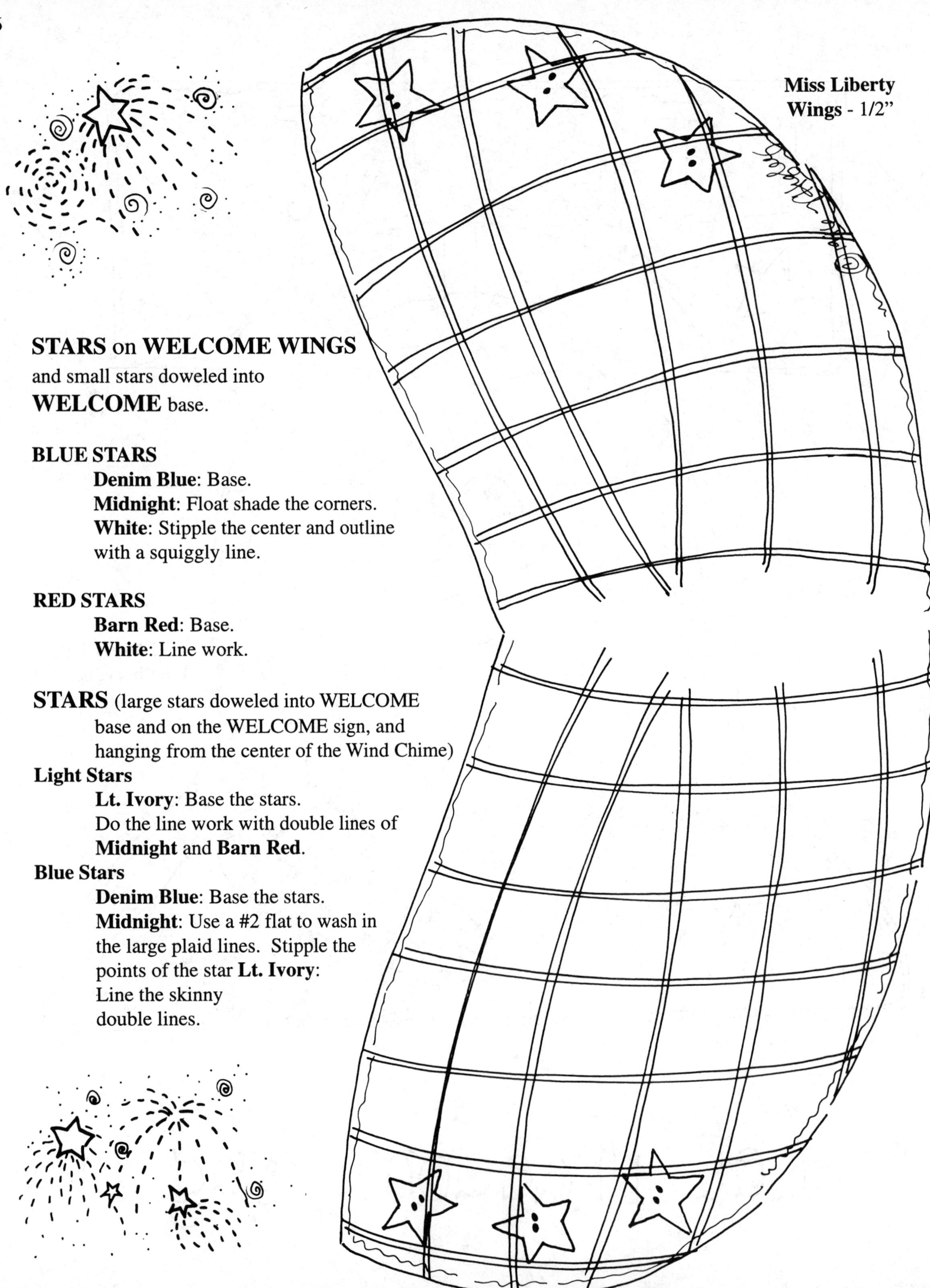

STARS on WELCOME WINGS

and small stars doweled into
WELCOME base.

BLUE STARS

Denim Blue: Base.
Midnight: Float shade the corners.
White: Stipple the center and outline
with a squiggly line.

RED STARS

Barn Red: Base.
White: Line work.

STARS (large stars doweled into WELCOME

base and on the WELCOME sign, and
hanging from the center of the Wind Chime)

Light Stars

Lt. Ivory: Base the stars.
Do the line work with double lines of
Midnight and **Barn Red**.

Blue Stars

Denim Blue: Base the stars.
Midnight: Use a #2 flat to wash in
the large plaid lines. Stipple the
points of the star **Lt. Ivory**:
Line the skinny
double lines.

FLAGS

Denim Blue: Base the blue field.
Midnight: Float shade the edges and lightly stipple the center area.
Light Ivory: Base the remaining area of the flag.
Barn Red: Base the red stripes.
White: Base the star and do the stitching on the blue field of the WELCOME flag.
Denim Blue: Float shade around the star and line the tiny stars and do the dots.
Straw: Undercoat the flag pole.
14 K Gold: Base the flag pole.

WIND CHIME - Finishing up

Black: Base the negative area.

Wind Chime Base

Denim Blue: Basecoat the base.
Midnight: Stipple the top and the edges.
Silver: Base the stars and do the line work on the edges.
Use your pen to outline the stars and do the line work.
Use wood glue to attach the bell to the base.
Varnish all the pieces with Krylon Matte Spray Finish.

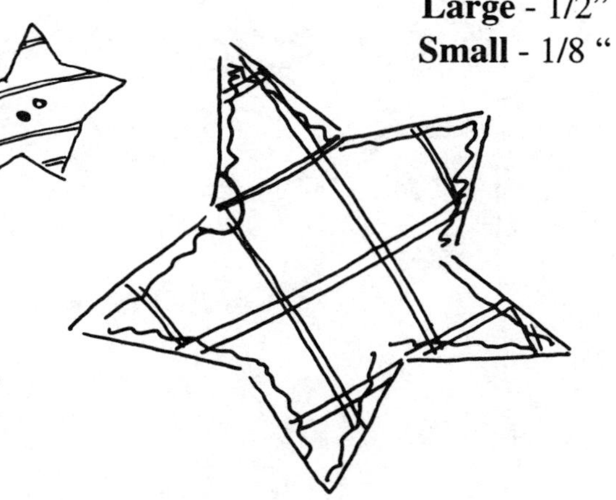

Miss Liberty's Stars
Large - 1/2"
Small - 1/8 "

PIPES

Cut and assemble according to the General Directions. I sprayed the pipes with Krylon Silver Metallic Enamel. I was pleasantly surprised at how easily it covered the pipes.

Attach 2 screw eyes to the top ends of the flag. Cut and curl 24" of wire around the handle of a brush and thread through the screw eyes. Bend the ends around and cut off any extra wire. Attach a screw eye to the bottom center of the base, the top and bottom of 1 blue star and the Lt. Ivory star and the top of the last Blue Star. Attach the stars to the base with the **Metallic Blue** Cording. Tie a knot in the end of each cord to prevent unraveling.

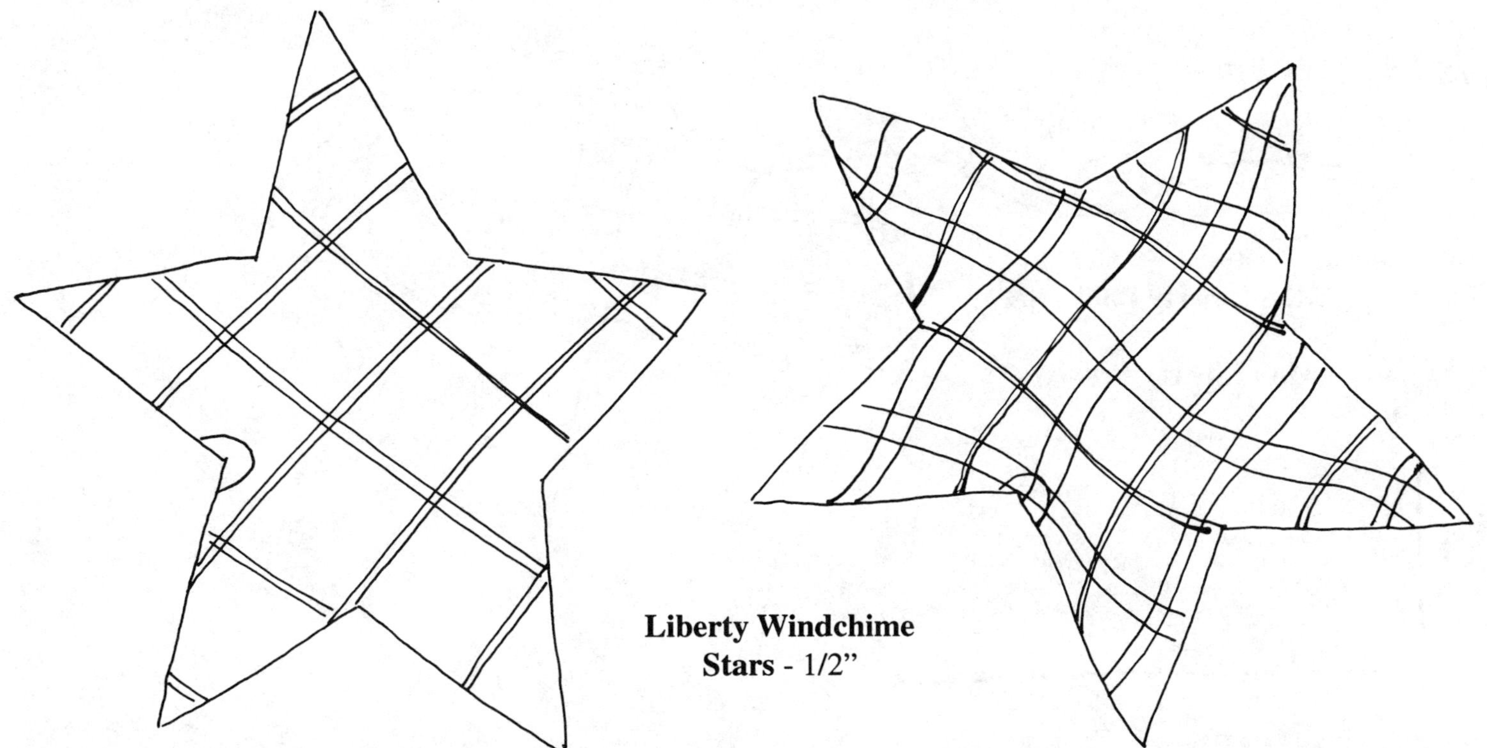

Liberty Windchime
Stars - 1/2"

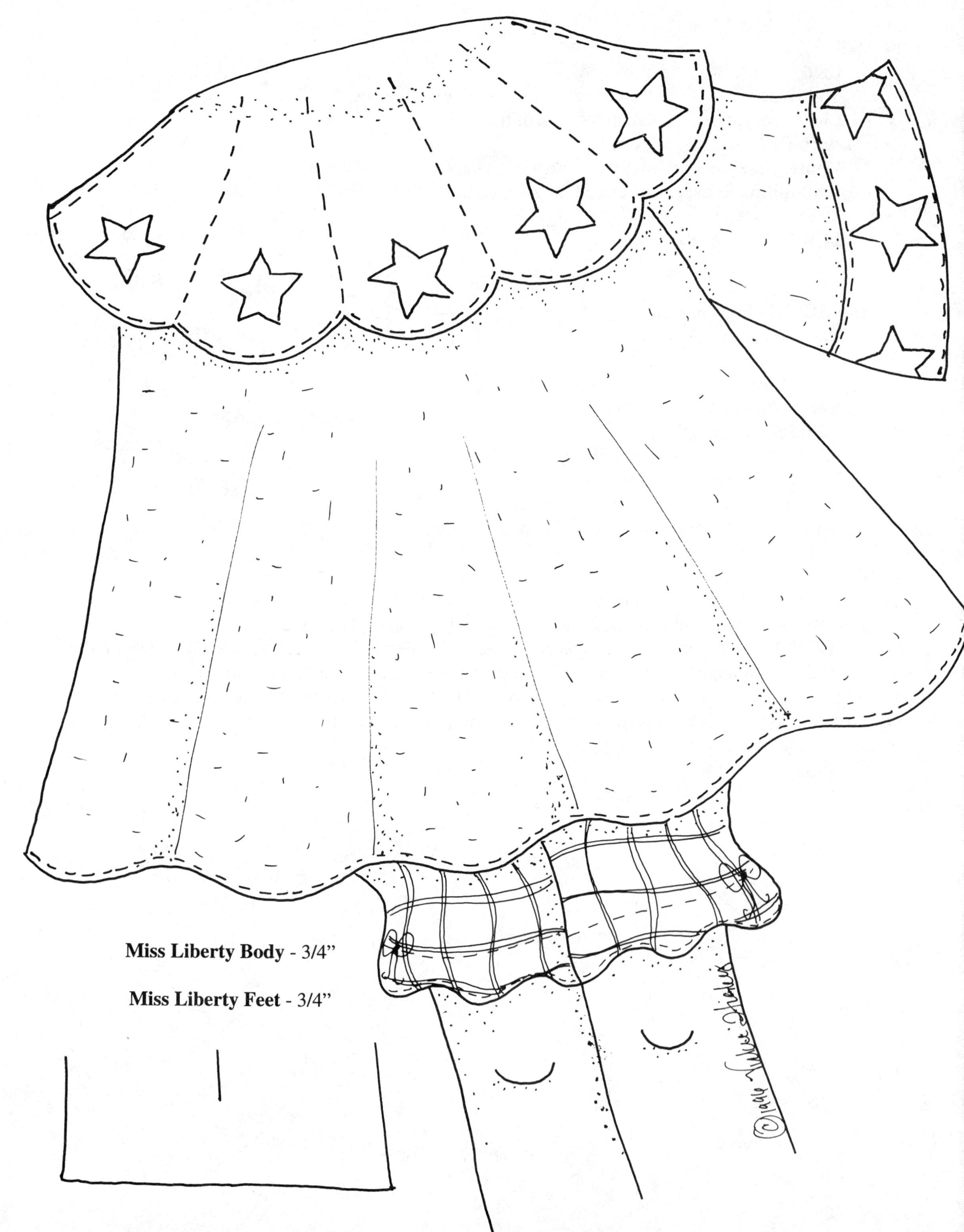
Miss Liberty Body - 3/4"
Miss Liberty Feet - 3/4"

MISS ANGEL of LIBERTY

(Follow the detail painting directions listed under the LIGHT FIRECRACKER for the wings and bloomers. The painting directions for the stars is under STARS).

Lt. Ivory: Base the bloomers and wings

FACE, HANDS and LEGS

Santa's Flesh: Basecoat.
Medium Flesh: Float shade the bottom sides of her face, around her eyes, and under the eye brows. Float shade her hands, feet and legs.
Barn Red: Base the mouth, and lightly float the nose.
Tangerine: Lightly stipple the very bottom of the bottom lip and the bottom of the top lip. Float Highlight those same areas.
Barn Red + a little **Black**: Palette blend lightly float shade the top of the top lip and underneath the top lip. Use a liner and pull tiny little lines in the lips.
White: Base the eyes, float highlight the chin.
Black: Base the pupils.
Denim Blue: Float shade the iris.
Midnight Blue: Float shade the iris again to deepen.

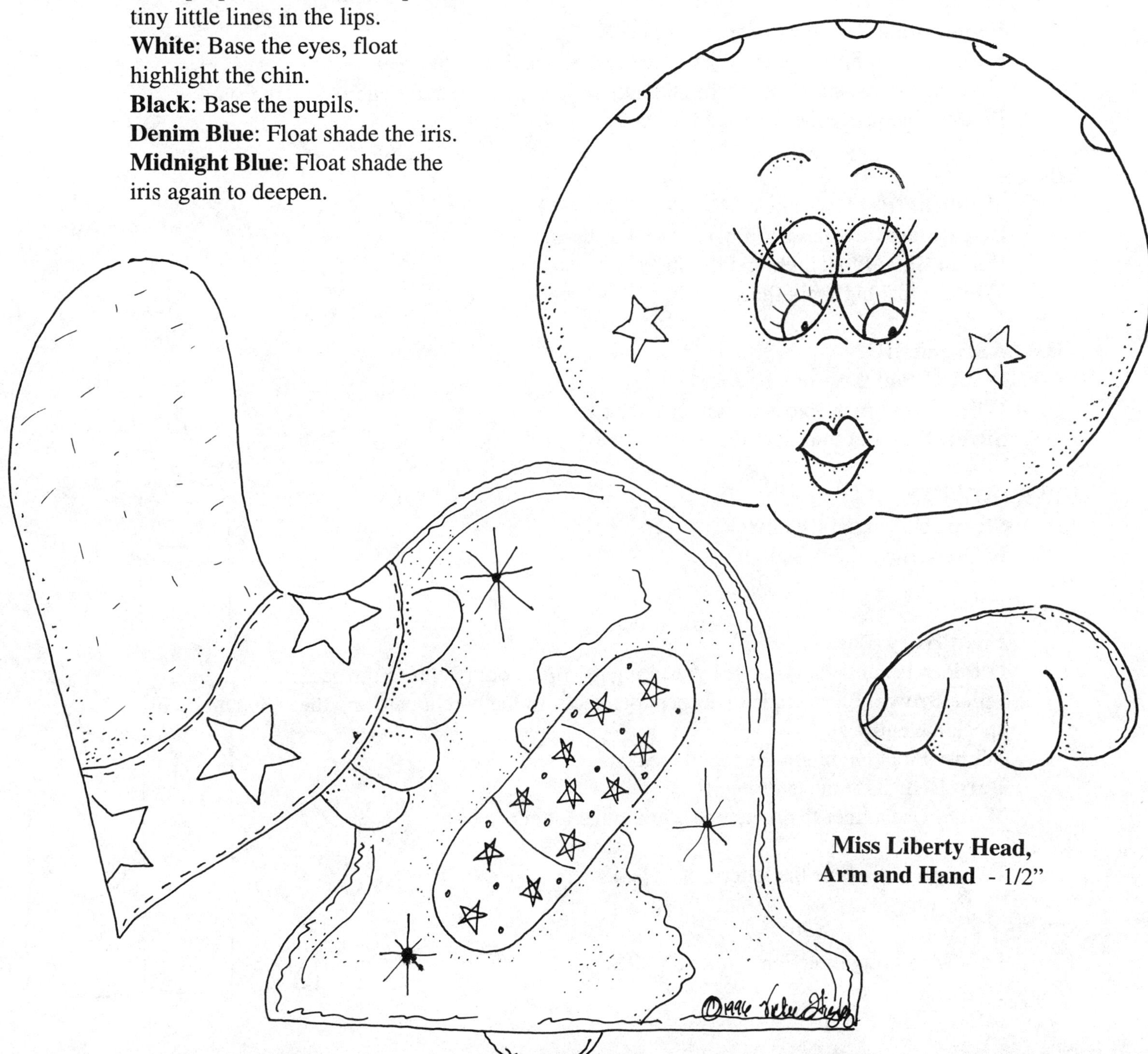

Miss Liberty Head, Arm and Hand - 1/2"

FACE, HANDS and LEGS Continued

White: Float highlight the tops of her knees, feet and fingers.
Barn Red: Stipple the cheeks.
Silver: Wash in the stars on her cheeks.
Black: Outline the eyes and eyebrows. I used a Loew-Cornell 7350 Round #2 brush to do the eyelashes.

DRESS

Barn Red: Base the dress.
Candy Bar: Float shade.
White: Lightly stipple the center of the sleeves and dress sections. Use your liner to do the pattern on the dress.

COLLAR and CUFFS

Denim Blue: Base the collar and the cuffs.
Midnight: Lightly stipple over the denim area leaving light areas.
Silver: Base the stars and do the stitching (if you prefer, cut a stencil to do the stars).
Black: Line under the collar and the cuffs.

SHOES

Midnight: Base the shoes.
Black: Base the soles and float shade the shoes.
Denim Blue: Float highlight the shoes.
White: Float highlight the soles.

THE BASE and SIGN

Denim Blue: Basecoat the base.
White: Dry brush across the top of the base.
Silver: Base the stars and do the stroke work on the sides of the base.

STAR DOWELS

Straw: Undercoat the dowels.
K Gold: Base the dowels.

SIGN

Light Ivory: Base the sign.
Old Parchment: Float shade by walking the floats out (Refer to the pattern).
Spice Brown: Float shade to deepen the cracks in the parchment, and the rolled area. Fly speck the entire sign.
White: Float Highlight the rolled area.
Barn Red: Base the lettering.
White: Use a liner to do the line work in the letters.

Use a pen to outline the letters.

STARS

Follow painting directions under STARS.

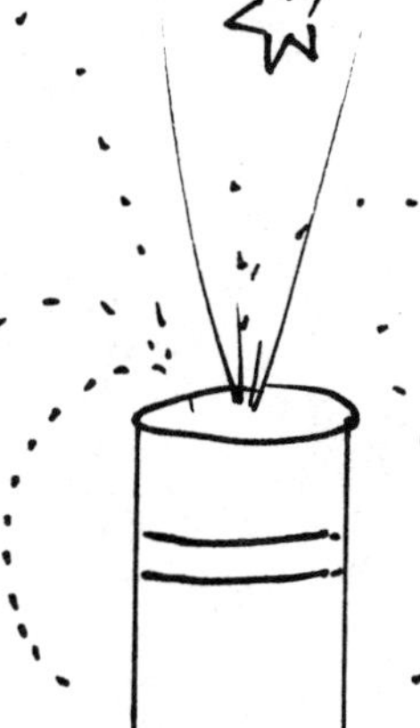
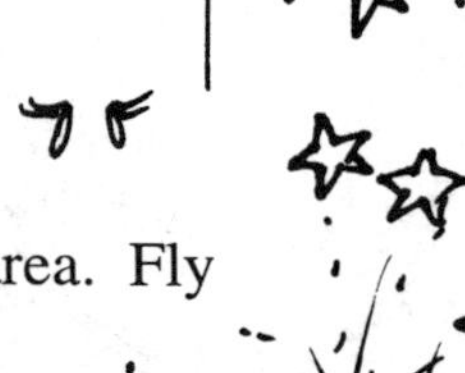
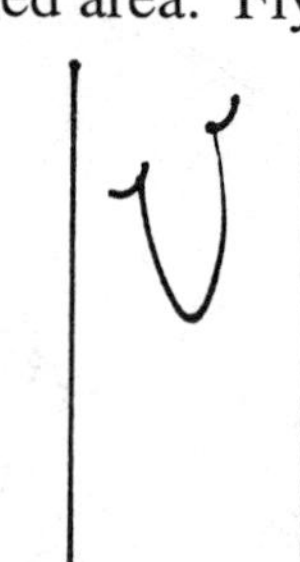
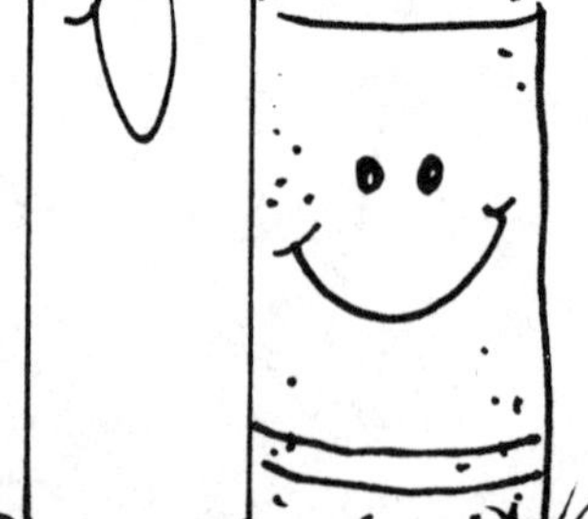

WEATHER VANE
Firecrackers

BLUE FIRECRACKER
Denim Blue: Base coat
Midnight: Float shade around the firecracker and inside the top edge. Use a #2 flat to wash in the wide plaid stripes.
Light Ivory: Lightly stipple the center area and the very top. Use a liner to do the double skinny lines.
Base the rest of the firecracker area **Lt. Ivory**. This keeps the red firecracker from getting too dark.

RED FIRECRACKER
Barn Red: Wash over the Light Ivory using several light washes. Be sure to dry thoroughly between coats. Use a blow drier to speed up this process.
Candy Bar: Float shade.
Light Ivory: Lightly stipple the face area.
White: Base the eyes.
Black: Dot the pupils and line the mouth.
Denim Blue: Float shade the iris.
White: Dot the eyes.
Black: Outline the eyes and do the eyelashes.

LIGHT FIRECRACKER
Old Parchment: Float Shade.
White: Stipple the center area.
Midnight: Line the double vertical lines.
Barn Red: Line the horizontal double lines.

Use your pen to do the outlining.
Varnish all the pieces.

Cut the star garland into twelve 3" pieces.
Fold each piece in half and insert into the
top of the firecrackers. Twist the tops together.

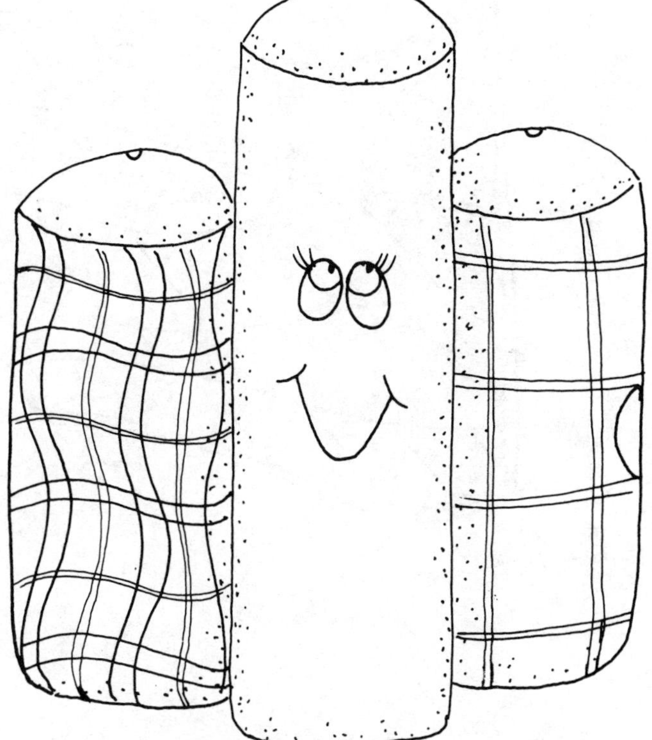

Weathervane Firecrackers - 3/4”

Attach the cording to the dowels. On two of the dowels I used 2 silver and 1 blue cord and reversed it for the other two dowels. Tie a bow at the top. Cut the cords to stagger the lengths and then tie a knot in the end of each cord.

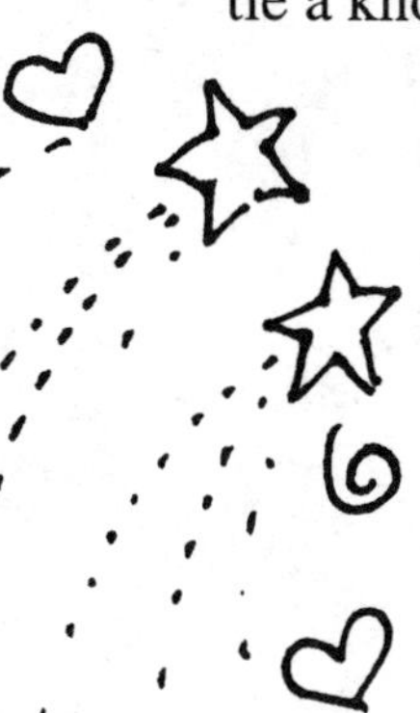
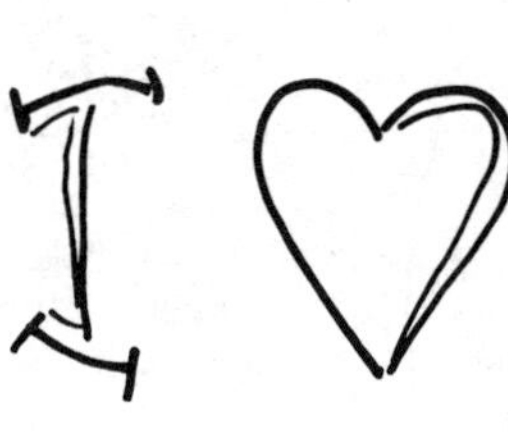
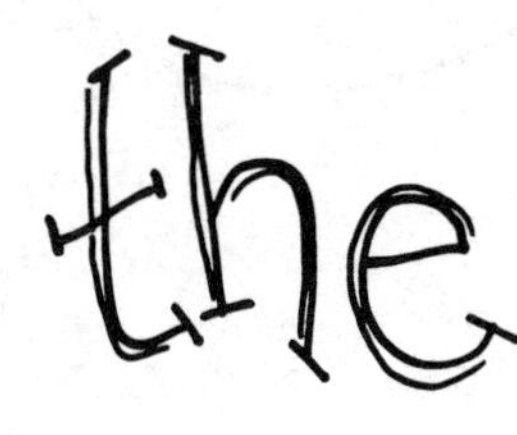
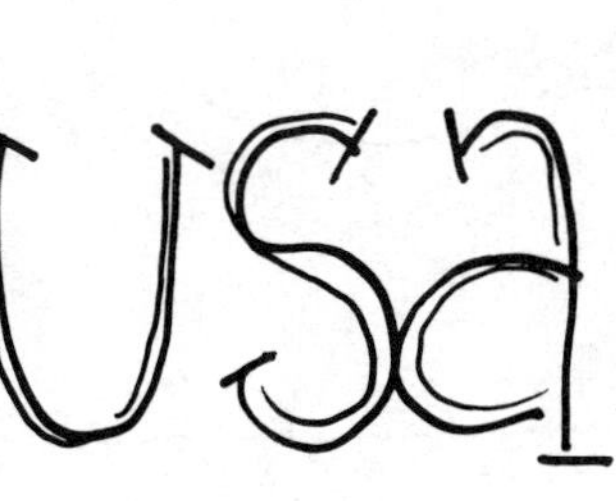
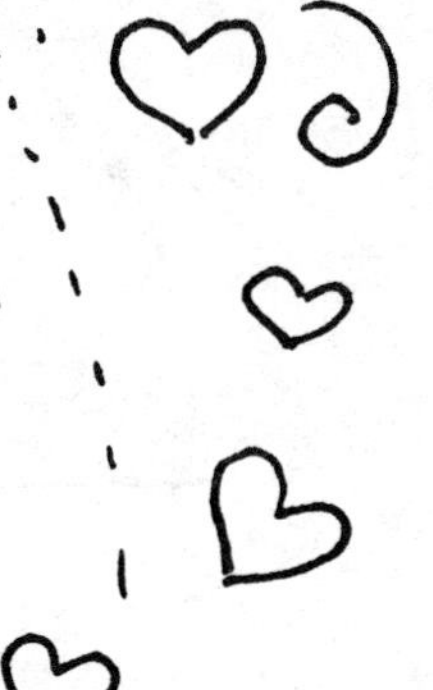

FINISHING UP

Use wood glue to attach all the pieces together. Varnish with Krylon Matte Spray Finish. Attach screw eyes to the sign and base. Cut two 12" pieces of wire. Thread the wire through the screw eyes and curl the ends by wrapping the wire around a brush. Use a piece of blue and silver cording to tie bows. Hot glue to the base.

HAIR

Hot glue the 2 1/2" pieces of jute into the holes. When set, tie on 2 pieces of fabric to each piece of jute. Tie a fabric bow for the bang and hot glue on.

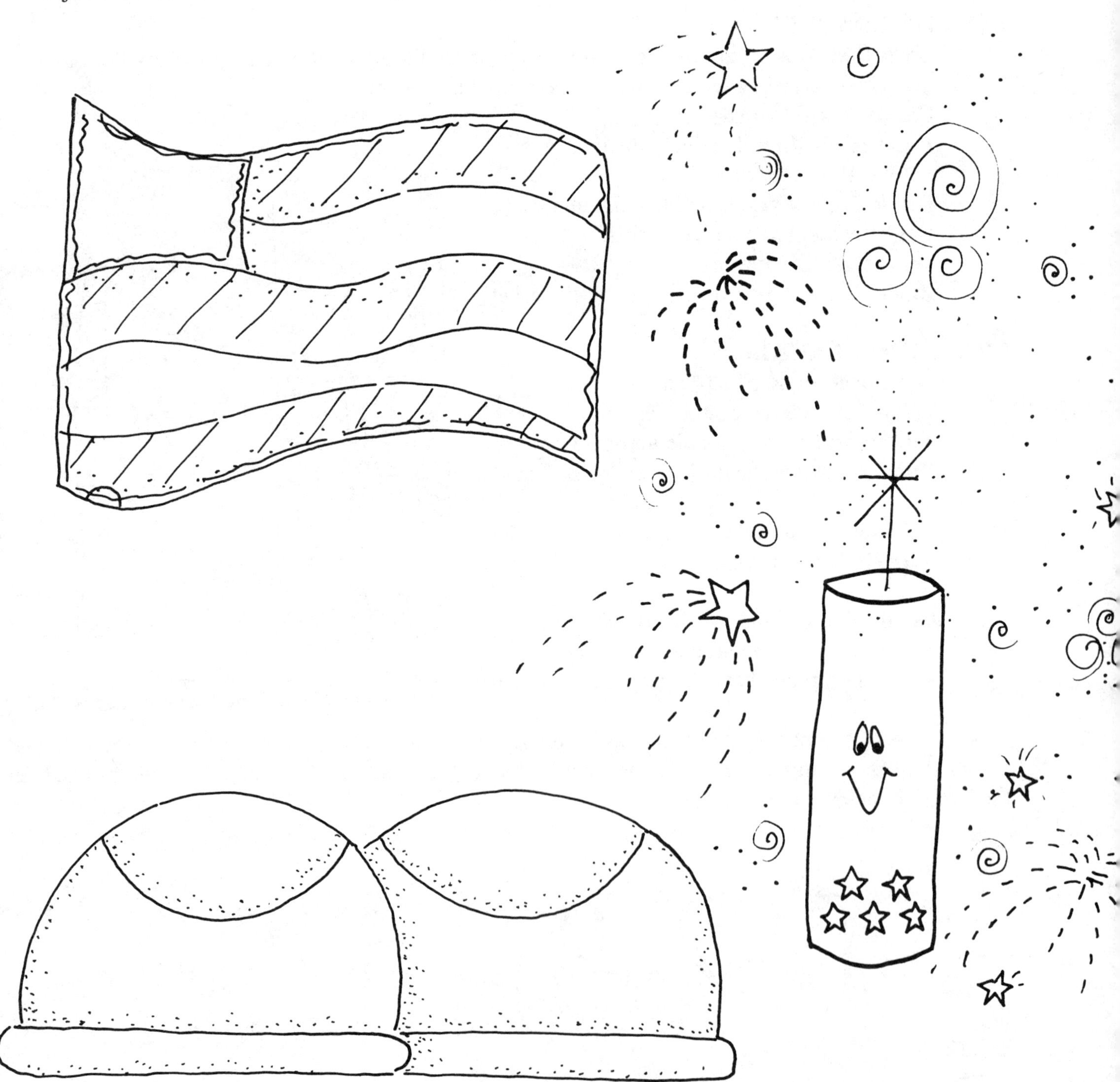

Susan Scheewe Publications Inc.

13435 N.E. Whitaker Way Portland, Or. 97230 PH (503)254-9100 FAX (503)252-9508

WATERCOLOR BOOKS

Vol. 20	"Simply Country Watercolors" by Susan Scheewe Brown	257	$9.50	___
Vol. 21	"Simply Watercolor" by Susan Scheewe Brown.....T.V. Book	260	$11.95	___
Vol. 23	"Watercolor Step by Step" by Susan Scheewe Brown.....T.V. Book	294	$11.95	___
Vol. 24	"Introduction to Watercolor" by Susan Scheewe Brown.....T.V. Book	314	$11.95	___
Vol. 25	"Watercolors Anyone Can Paint" by Susan Scheewe Brown...T.V. Book	325	$11.95	___
NEW Vol. 26	"Watercolor - The Garden Scene" by Susan Scheewe Brown... T.V. Book	339	$11.95	___
NEW Vol. 27	"Watercolor Landscapes" by Susan Scheewe Brown.....T.V. Book	360	$11.95	___
Vol. 4	"Enjoy Watercolor" by Ellie Cook	210	$7.50	___
Vol. 6	"Watercolor Memories" by Ellie Cook	246	$9.50	___
Vol. 7	"Watercolor Journey" by Ellie Cook.....*NEW*	381	$9.50	___
Vol. 3	"Watercolor Made Easy 3" by Kathy George	301	$9.50	___
Vol. 1	"The Way I Started" by Gary Hawk	120	$6.00	___
Vol. 2	"Anyone Can Watercolor" by Ken Johnson	118	$6.50	___
Vol. 1	"Watercolor Fun & Easy" by Beverly Kaiser	243	$7.50	___
Vol. 1	"Flowers, Ribbon and Lace in Watercolor" by Linda McCulloch	280	$9.50	___
Vol. 7	"Watercolor Charms" by Sharon Rachal...*NEW*	376	$9.50	___

PEN & INK BOOKS / COLORED PENCIL BOOKS

Vol. 6	"Journey of Memories" by Claudia Nice	166	$6.50	___
Vol. 7	"Scenes from Seasons Past" by Claudia Nice	183	$9.50	___
Vol. 8	"Taste of Summer" by Claudia Nice	223	$9.50	___
Vol. 9	"Familiar Faces" by Claudia Nice	284	$9.50	___
Vol. 2	"Colored Pencil Made Easy" by Jane Wunder	242	$7.50	___
Vol. 3	"The Beauty of Colored Pencil and Ink Drawing" by Jane Wunder	259	$7.50	___
Vol. 4	"Watercolor, Pen and Ink" by Jane Wunder	357	$9.50	___

VIDEOS BY SUSAN SCHEEWE BROWN

"Paintings For The Holidays" 1 Hour		$24.95	___
"Fabric Painting Fun" 1 Hour		$24.95	___
"Watercolor Techniques" 1 Hour	S8226	$19.95	___
"Painting Projects" Watercolor 3 Hours	S8224	$49.95	___
"Scheewe Art Workshop I" 13-1/2 HR Shows On 4 Tapes	S8225	$69.95	___
"Scheewe Art Workshop II" 13-1/2 HR Shows On 4 Tapes	S8223	$69.95	___

NAME _______________________

____

ADDRESS _______________________

____

CITY/STATE/ZIP _______________________

____

PH(   ) _______________________

VISA _______________________

M/C _______________________

EXP. DATE _______________________

SHIPPING $ _______________________

SHIP TO _______________________

____

OILS BOOKS

Vol. 1	"His and Hers" by Susan Scheewe	101	$6.50	___
Vol. 7	"Paint 'n Patch" by Susan Scheewe	107	$5.50	___
Vol. 11	"I Love To Paint" by Susan Scheewe	111	$6.50	___
Vol. 14	"Enjoy Painting Animals" by Susan Scheewe	114	$6.50	___
Vol. 19	"Gift Of Painting" by Susan Scheewe O/AC/WC	230	$9.50	___
Vol. 1	"Western Images" by Becky Anthony	186	$6.50	___
Vol. 5	"Soft Petals" by Georgia Bartlett	171	$6.50	___
Vol. 6	"Painting Fantasy Flowers" by Georgia Bartlett	215	$7.50	___
Vol. 8	"Petals" by Georgia Bartlett	317	$9.50	___
Vol. 9	"Floral Medley" by Georgia Bartlett *NEW*	344	$9.50	___
Vol. 3	"Barnscapes & More" by Donna Bell	218	$9.50	___
Vol. 4	"Countryscapes" by Donna Bell	249	$9.50	___
Vol. 5	"Painter to Painter" by Donna Bell	263	$9.50	___
Vol. 6	"Landscapes With Acrylics & Oil" by Donna Bell	282	$9.50	___
Vol. 1	"Natures Palette" by Carol Binford.....O/AC	248	$9.50	___
Vol. 2	"Oil Painting The Easy Way" by Bill Blackman	337	$9.50	___
Vol. 3	"Lighted Windows & Gardens" by Bill Blackman...*NEW*	355	$9.50	___
Vol. 1	"Mini Mini More" by Terri and Nancy Brown	150	$6.50	___
Vol. 2	"Mini Mini More" by Terri and Nancy Brown	151	$6.50	___
Vol. 4	"Heritage Trails" by Terri and Nancy Brown	169	$6.50	___
Vol. 6	"Garden Trails" by Terri and Nancy Brown	283	$9.50	___
Vol. 7	"More Garden Trails" by Terri and Nancy Brown...*NEW*	368	$9.50	___
Vol. 2	"Windows of My World" by Jackie Claflin	181	$9.50	___
Vol. 3	"Windows of My World 3" by Jackie Claflin	303	$9.50	___
Vol. 4	"Windows Of My World 4" by Jackie Claflin.....*NEW*	359	$9.50	___
Vol. 4	"Expressions In Oil" by Delores Egger	239	$7.50	___
Vol. 1	"Victorian Days" by Gloria Gaffney	240	$9.50	___
Vol. 2	"Days of Heaven" by Gloria Gaffney	252	$9.50	___
Vol. 6	"The Sky's The Limit" by Jean Green.....*NEW*	372	$9.50	___
Vol. 3	"Nature's Beauty" by Bill Huffaker	177	$6.50	___
Vol. 1	"In Full Bloom" by Susan Jenkins	313	$9.50	___
Vol. 1	"Backroads of My Memory" by Geri Kisner	225	$9.50	___
Vol. 2	"Backroads of My Memory" by Geri Kisner	245	$9.50	___
Vol. 1	"Ducks and Geese" by Jean Lyles	172	$6.50	___
Vol. 1	"Raining Cats & Dogs" by Todd Mallett	304	$9.50	___
Vol. 1	"Pathway To Painting" by Lee McGowan	281	$9.50	___
Vol. 2	"Another Path To Follow" by Lee McGowen	328	$9.50	___
Vol. 1	"Bitterroot Backroads" by Glenice Moore-Nickel	330	$9.50	___
Vol. 2	"Bitterroot Backroads 2" by Glenice Moore-Nickel	340	$9.50	___
Vol. 3	"Bitterroot Backroads 3" by Glenice Moore-Nickel.*NEW*	369	$9.50	___
Vol. 1	"Stepping Stones" by Judy Nutter	121	$6.50	___
Vol. 1	"Painting with Paulson" by Buck Paulson	343	$11.95	___
Vol. 1	"Rustic Charms" by Sharon Rachal	175	$6.50	___
Vol. 2	"Rustic Charms II" by Sharon Rachal	199	$9.50	___
Vol. 3	"Rustic Charms III" by Sharon Rachal	217	$6.50	___
Vol. 4	"Rustic Charms IV" by Sharon Rachal	238	$7.50	___
Vol. 5	"Rustic Charms V, Florals" by Sharon Rachal	261	$9.50	___
Vol. 1	"Painting Flowers With Augie" by Augie Reis	152	$6.50	___
Vol. 3	"Realistic Technique" by Judy Sleight	341	$9.50	___
Vol. 2	"Soft & Misty Paintings" by Kathy Snider	229	$9.50	___
Vol. 4	"Friends We've Known" by Gene Waggoner	187	$7.50	___
Vol. 5	"Friends Are Forever" by Gene Waggoner	231	$7.50	___
Vol. 1	"Fantasy Folk" by Don Weed	123	$6.50	___
Vol. 2	"Painting The Clowns" by Don Weed	124	$6.50	___
Vol. 1	"Something Special For Everyone" by Mildred Yeiser	158	$6.50	___
Vol. 2	"Something Special For Everyone" by Mildred Yeiser	178	$6.50	___
Vol. 5	"Soft & Gentle Paintings" by Mildred Yeiser	268	$9.50	___

Susan Scheewe Publications, Inc.

13435 N.E. Whitaker Way Portland, Or. 97230 PH (503)254-9100 FAX (503)252-9508

ACRYLIC BOOKS

Vol. 19	"Gift of Painting" by Susan Scheewe	230	$9.50___
Vol. 1	"Painting It's Our Bag" by Bev Hink/Susan Scheewe	193	$9.50___
Vol. 4	"Keepsake Sampler" by Susan & Camille Scheewe	200	$9.50___
Vol. 1	"Loving You" by Susan & Camille Scheewe	244	$9.50___
Vol. 1	"Keepsakes For The Holidays" by C. Stempel & S. Scheewe	286	$9.50___
Vol. 1	"Country Heartworks" by Reed Baxter	352	$9.50___
Vol. 2	'Country Heartworks 2" by Reed Baxter....*NEW	365	$9.50___
Vol. 1	"Kids And Water" by Joyce Benner	234	$9.50___
Vol. 2	"The Flower Market" by Joyce Benner	319	$9.50___
Vol. 2	"Country Fixin's - Sunflower Friends" by Rhonda Caldwell	321	$9.50___
Vol. 3	"Country Fixin's - For All Seasons" by Rhonda Caldwell	332	$9.50___
Vol. 4	"Country Fixin's 4" by Rhonda Caldwell...*NEW	364	$9.50___
Vol. 1	"Country Celebration" by Tammy Christensen...*NEW	378	$9.50___
Vol. 1	"A Painters Garden" by Jane Dillon	354	$9.50___
Vol. 1	"Santas and Sams" by Bobi Dolara	258	$9.50___
Vol. 2	"Vintage Peace" by Bobi Dolara	270	$9.50___
Vol. 1	"Floral Designs" by Carol Empet	312	$9.50___
Vol. 2	"Floral Designs 2" by Carol Empet	338	$9.50___
Vol. 3	"Floral Portraits" by Carol Empet	358	$9.50___
Vol. 1	"Briar Patch" by Sandy Fochler...*NEW	380	$9.50___
Vol. 1	"Romantically Tole Bauernmalerei" by Sherry Gall	311	$9.50___
Vol. 1	"Holiday Gathering" by Angie Hupp	267	$9.50___
Vol. 3	"Heavenly Gathering" by Angie Hupp	320	$9.50___
Vol. 1	"Happy Heart, Happy Home" by Cathy Jones	241	$9.50___
Vol. 1	"Pickets & Pastimes" by Marie & Jim King	329	$9.50___
Vol. 2	"Pickets & Pastimes 2, Heart of The Seasons" by M. & J. King	348	$9.50___
Vol. 3	"Pickets & Pastimes 3, Feathered Ends" by M. & J. King...*NEW	385	$9.50___
Vol. 1	"For Me & My House" by Myrna King...*NEW	370	$9.50___
Vol. 1	"Huckleberry Horse" by Hanna Long	269	$9.50___
Vol. 2	"Love Lives Here" by Mary Lynn Lewis	185	$6.50___
Vol. 3	"Love Lives Here" by Mary Lynn Lewis	195	$6.50___
Vol. 1	"Special Welcomes" by Corinne Miller	287	$9.50___
Vol. 2	"Special Welcomes" by Corinne Miller	298	$9.50___
Vol. 3	"Special Welcomes #3, Crazy About Crafting" by Corinne Miller	309	$9.50___
Vol. 4	"Special Welcomes #4 Farm-N-Friends" by Corinne Miller	324	$9.50___
Vol. 5	"Special Welcomes #5 All Wrapped Up" by Corinne Miller	333	$9.50___
Vol. 6	"Special Welcomes #6 Crop Keepers" by Corinne Miller	347	$9.50___
Vol. 1	"Change With The Seasons, Wire Loops" by Joanna Miller	331	$9.50___
Vol. 1	"Fruit & Flower Fantasies" by Joyce Morrison	277	$9.50___
Vol. 2	"Fruit & Flower Fantasies 2" by Joyce Morrison...*NEW	382	$9.50___
Vol. 1	"Whimsical Critters" by Lori Ohlson	227	$7.50___
Vol. 2	"Sunflower Farm" by Lori Ohlson	326	$9.50___
Vol. 1	"Holiday Medley" by Nina Owens	265	$9.50___
Vol. 2	"Another Holiday Medley" by Nina Owens	296	$9.50___
Vol. 1	"Oh Those Little Rascals" by Diane Permenter	247	$9.50___
Vol. 6	"Acrylic Charms" by Sharon Rachal	305	$9.50___
Vol. 1	"Forever In My Heart" by Diane Richards.....AC/Fabric	188	$6.50___
Vol. 2	"Memories In My Heart" by Diane Richards.....AC/Fabric	189	$6.50___
Vol. 3	"Forever In My Heart II" by Diane Richards.....AC/Fabric	205	$9.50___
Vol. 6	"Angels In My Stocking" by Diane Richards	254	$9.50___
Vol. 7	"Nostalgic Dreams" by Diane Richards	273	$9.50___
Vol. 8	"Angel Kisses" by Diane Richards	346	$9.50___
Vol. 1	"Country Fun For Chistmas" by Tina Rodriguez	367	$9.50___
Vol. 2	"Country Fun 2" by Tina Rodriguez...*NEW	383	$9.50___
Vol. 1	"Second Time Around" by Sally Sauermilch	297	$9.50___
Vol. 1	"Holiday Hangarounds" by Marsha Sellers	327	$9.50___
Vol. 1	"Creations In Canvas...and More" by Carol Spooner	256	$9.50___
Vol. 1	"Gran's Garden" by Ros Stallcup	295	$9.50___
Vol. 2	"Another Gran's Garden" by Ros Stallcup	315	$9.50___
Vol. 3	"Gran's Garden & House" by Ros Stallcup	334	$9.50___
Vol. 4	"Gran's Garden Party" by Ros Stallcup	345	$9.50___
Vol. 4	"Gran's Treasures" by Ros Stallcup	363	$9.50___
Vol. 1	"Blackberry Hollow" by Margaret Steed...*NEW	384	$9.50___
Vol. 1	"Christmas Greetings from the Cottage" by Chris Stokes	336	$9.50___
Vol. 1	"Home Sweet Home" by Wendy Guinn and Leah Sukraw...*NEW	377	$9.50___
Vol. 1	"Christmas Visions" by Max Terry	278	$9.50___
Vol. 3	"Painting Clay Pot-pourri" by Max Terry	310	$9.50___
Vol. 4	"The Nesting Place" by Max Terry...*NEW	373	$9.50___
Vol. 1	"Country Primitives" by Maxine Thomas	274	$9.50___
Vol. 2	"Country Primitives 2" by Maxine Thomas	300	$9.50___
Vol. 3	"Country Primitives 3" by Maxine Thomas	322	$9.50___
Vol. 4	"Country Primitives 4" by Maxine Thomas...*NEW	350	$9.50___
Vol. 1	"Rise & Shine" by Jolene Thompson	214	$6.50___
Vol. 2	"Garden Gate" by Jolene Thompson	250	$9.50___
Vol. 5	"Count Your Blessings" by Chris Thornton	213	$9.50___
Vol. 6	"Share Your Blessings" by Chris Thornton	226	$9.50___
Vol. 7	"Blessings" by Chris Thornton	255	$9.50___
Vol. 8	"Christmas Blessings" by Chris Thornton	266	$9.50___
Vol. 9	"Blessings For The Home" by Chris Thornton	275	$9.50___
Vol. 10	"Bazaar Blessings" by Chris Thornton	299	$9.50___
Vol. 11	"Painted Blessings" by Chris Thornton	323	$9.50___
Vol. 12	"Family Blessings" by Chris Thornton	349	$9.50___
Vol. 13	"Garden Blessings" by Chris Thornton	356	$9.50___
Vol. 14	"Friendship Blessings" by Chris Thorton	371	$9.50___
Vol. 15	"Multitude of Blessings" by Chris Thorton...*NEW	379	$9.50___
Vol. 1	"Watermelon Wedges and Rustic Edges" by Lorinne Thurlow	342	$9.50___
Vol. 2	"Watermelon Wedges and Rustic Edges 2" by L. Thurlow	353	$9.50___
Vol. 3	"Watermelon Wedges and Rustic Edges 3" by L. Thurlow	362	$9.50___
Vol. 1	"Barnyard Friends" by Lou Ann Trice	306	$9.50___
Vol. 2	"Farmer and Friends" by Lou Ann Trice...*NEW	366	$9.50___
Vol. 5	"Daydreams & Sweet Shirts II" by Don & Lynn Weed	208	$9.50___
Vol. 1	"Connie's Favorite Old-Time Labels" by Connie Williams	335	$9.50___
Vol. 2	"Connie's Garden Seed Packets" by Connie Williams	351	$9.50___
Vol. 1	"Floral Fabrics and Watercolor" by Sally Williams	262	$9.50___
Vol. 1	"A Time For Giving" by Evelyn Wright	308	$9.50___

NAME _______________________________

ADDRESS _______________________________

____

CITY/STATE/ZIP _______________________________

____

PH ( ) _______________________________

VISA _______________________________

M/C _______________________________

EXP. DATE _______________________________

SHIPPING $ _______________________________

SHIP TO: _______________________________

____

****
SHIPPING &
HANDLING
CHARGES
Add $2.50 for the First Book for shipping and handling.

Add $1.50 per each additional book.

Please Add $3.00 for handling & postage. PER TAPES. Sorry we must have a "NO REFUND - NO RETURN" policy.

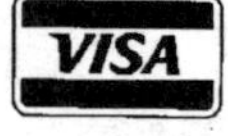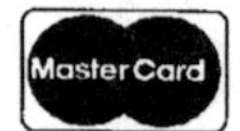

PRICES SUBJECT TO CHANGE WITHOUT NOTICE

FOR MORE INFORMATION ON BOOKS OR SUPPLIES CALL OR WRITE US

WE ARE ALWAYS GLAD TO HEAR FROM YOU!

1-8-97